Outsmarting Your Kids Online
A Safety Handbook for Overwhelmed Parents

Amber Mac
Michael Bazzell

Outsmarting Your Kids Online
A Safety Handbook for Overwhelmed Parents

Published: May 2016

Project Editors: Y. Varallo & L. Killian

Library of Congress Cataloging-in-Publication Data:
Application submitted

ISBN-13: 978-0692682692

ISBN-10: 0692682694

Contents

About Us

Amber Mac

Amber Mac is a bestselling author, TV host, keynote speaker, and technology entrepreneur. She started her career at Razorfish during the dot-com boom in San Francisco in 1999. Amber has reported on technology news and trends for more than 12 years for CNN, G4TechTV, CBS, CTV, CBC, The Marilyn Denis Show, Fast Company, The Globe & Mail, and many other media organizations.

She has keynoted more than 300 events worldwide teaching audiences about the latest social media and technology trends. She also runs a digital agency called Konnekt, that works with clients ranging from Tony Robbins to Microsoft to W Network. Her first book, *Power Friending*, was a national bestseller (Portfolio / New York). Amber's 7-year-old son is a savvy Internet user.

Michael Bazzell

Michael Bazzell spent 18 years as a government computer crime investigator. During the majority of that time, he was assigned to the FBI's Cyber Crimes Task Force where he focused on open source intelligence and computer crime investigations. As an active investigator for multiple organizations, he has been involved in numerous high-tech criminal investigations including online child solicitation, child abduction, kidnapping, cold-case homicide, terrorist threats, and high level computer intrusions. He has trained thousands of individuals in the use of his investigative techniques.

Michael currently works and resides in Washington, D.C. He also serves as the technical advisor for the television hacker drama *Mr. Robot* on the USA network. His books *Open Source Intelligence Techniques* and *Hiding from the Internet* have been best sellers in both the United States and Europe. They are used by several government agencies as training manuals for intelligence gathering and securing personal information.

Chapter One
Today's Landscape

The Rise of The Screeners

In the fall of 2011, a YouTube video made the rounds to almost five million homes featuring a one-year-old child flipping through a magazine, attempting to scroll down the page with a practiced two-finger swipe. As she presses on each glossy image, including a perfume advertisement, she is visibly annoyed that nothing electronic happens. The little girl pushes down on her leg to make sure her finger is still working, and then leans forward to get her trusted iPad back in her tiny hands.

While this video, which is titled "A Magazine is an iPad That Does Not Work" is entertaining, the comments section is where the real story unfolds. It's not the story of this tiny person, but instead we see (mostly) adults arguing with each other about technology: the good, the bad, and the ugly. One person blames the baby's new habit on Steve Jobs; another says the parents should be ashamed of themselves; and another questions how this girl could possibly turn out to be a normal human being (what, with this demon gadget and all at her fingertips).

We are fooling ourselves if we think this girl is the exception. The American Academy of Pediatrics says that 36 percent of children under age one have touched some sort of screen. As they explain, by age two, most toddlers are using mobile devices. If a newborn could remember the first thing she sees when she enters her brand new world, it would probably be a parent's camera phone locked squarely on her little face. Like it or not, we spend our lives glued to technology, so it's only natural that children follow suit.

However, as kids grow up, they're not just following suit. They're adapting more quickly than we ever imagined (or, let's be honest, more quickly than we ever could). We are living during a unique time when we aren't properly equipped to handle the questions kids are asking; in fact, we are frequently turning to them to learn how all these shiny new things actually work. In 2014, the *Journal of Communication* found that 30-40 percent of parents were taught how to use a computer and the Internet by their children. When kids hit the teen years, their desire to help adults learn wanes. While this is the time when Mom and Dad need to assume a strong Internet mentor type role in the home, many aren't able to keep up with what their children are doing online; yet, there is probably no better time than now that it matters more that they do.

The Risks and Our Children

The American Academy of Pediatrics recently recommended that there should be absolutely no exposure to screens for children younger than two, but today they are working toward a more moderate view on this with heightened awareness that this is no longer realistic. New guidelines are expected in late 2016. This is just an example of how we're doing children a big disservice. Parental guidelines and parental rules aren't in sync and up-to-date with the pace of modern technology innovation. Whether it's an association, a school, or a parent, it's nearly impossible to stick to a long-term plan that accounts for the exponential growth of computers and the Internet. This means flexibility and adaptation are key success factors when parenting in the digital age.

With technology moving so quickly, it's also difficult to recognize the risks our children face at every stage of childhood. Within this book we'll talk about children throughout the following three stages: preschool (ages 3-5), preteen (ages 6-12), and teen (ages 13-18). Each group faces very different risks when it comes to their experiences online.

Within the youngest group of the three stages, the risks are perhaps less dangerous safety-wise, but good habits start here. For many of these preschoolers the problem is not their Internet habits, but their parents' bad online habits. Recent research from *The Parent Zone* discovered that moms and dads post an average of 973 photos of their kids online before their children turn five. This is a staggering number of pictures that could jeopardize your child's privacy later in life, or on more rare occasions, his or her safety. In Chapter Eight we will discuss all of these potential issues, and in Chapter Ten we'll address how parents can work smarter to protect these young children and provide guidance along the way.

The preteen group spans a number of years. Before your children hit double digits, chances are that you are monitoring some of what they're doing online. Since they are probably most often on a family computer or tablet, this is a bit easier to manage. When your children get smartphones, the risks increase dramatically. If this phone travels everywhere with them, which for safety reasons it probably does, there are plenty of ways you can still monitor what they're doing. When it comes to monitoring, there are some parents who are apprehensive about invading their children's privacy. We will address this further in Chapter Ten after we dive into specific social media and Internet risks.

For many of you reading this book, your children are in their teen years. This group is the most susceptible to a wide array of potential problems online. Whether they are experiencing bullying on Facebook; talking to strangers on anonymous apps; or simply glued to a smartphone 24-7, we will discuss some simple steps to keep them safe.

This is also the age group that leaves a detailed history online indicating where they've been, what they've been doing, and who they've been doing it with, without much regard for their privacy. In a CNN series focusing on 13-year-old kids online, "#Being13," they found that the heaviest users in the group checked their social media accounts more than 100 times a day. This group explained that they closely monitored social media to keep on top of their popularity status. In fact, 61 percent of them wanted to see if their posts were getting "likes" and 21 percent wanted to make sure no one was saying anything mean about them. "#Being13" also researched the teens' parents and found that 94 percent of them underestimated how much fighting was happening on social media. But for parents who did watch these accounts the closest, there was a positive effect. Yes, we can do better.

Throughout this book there are helpful how-tos and hacks to outsmart your kids online and empower you as a parent. Before getting further into some of these strategies, it's important that we define the difference between privacy and security in the context of your kids. These two terms are thrown around often throughout the media and within most online communities. Both privacy and security can have several different meanings to those concerned with either. We believe that you cannot have privacy without security and vice versa. This book will focus on several aspects of each. Our privacy and security concerns are each split into two categories: digital and physical.

Digital privacy concerns for most parents include threats related to a child's online activity or personal details. Sensitive online activity often includes social network posts, private messages to friends, and browsing history.

Personal details can include interests, hobbies, and identifiers such as a date of birth or Social Security number. It is vital to protect all of this. Consider what happened to Bobbi Duncan, a student at the University of Texas. In 2012, the 22-year-old joined Queer Chorus, a choir group consisting of homosexual members at her school. Doing so inadvertently exposed Ms. Duncan's sexuality to her nearly 200 Facebook friends and family by adding her to a Facebook discussion group about the choir. This was devastating to Bobbi at the time. The president of the choir had added her to the student organization's Facebook group. The president didn't know the service would automatically tell their Facebook friends that they were now members of the chorus consisting of gay students. Throughout the book, we will offer suggestions for securing online account privacy settings for optimal protection.

Physical privacy concerns of most parents include threats to a child's immediate surroundings. This could include unauthorized remote access to a webcam across the Internet or unapproved usage of your child's computer devices containing private information. A convincing example can be found in the lawsuit against the Lower Merion School District in Pennsylvania. In that case, a 15-year-old high school sophomore was disciplined at school for his behavior in his home. The school took action after a photograph had been secretly taken of him in his bedroom via the webcam in his school-issued laptop. Without telling its students, the school remotely accessed these laptops to secretly snap pictures of students in their own homes. They monitored their chat logs and recorded the websites they visited. The school then transmitted the snapshots to computers at the school, where school authorities reviewed them and shared the snapshots with others. In one published photo, the school had photographed the student in his bed. A small piece of electrical tape strategically placed over the small camera would have prevented this intrusive type of activity.

Digital security is the most overlooked safety element by busy parents. We all tend to purchase the latest gadgets for children without properly enabling optimal security settings. As an example, most cellular telephones do not include any type of unauthorized access prevention by default. Screen locks, encryption, and strong passwords are all optional. It is often only after a device is lost or stolen when these quick fixes are considered. Chapter Seven will explain easy modifications that can be made to better protect your child's computers, tablets, or cellular phones.

Physical security concerns are likely the most important to all parents. On very rare occasions, children are molested or abducted by individuals who they met online. Chapter Eight highlights warning signs of targeted physical attacks toward your child. By understanding the common avenues that predators will use to "groom" children, you can proactively monitor, identify, and report suspicious behavior. Michael investigated criminal child solicitations and abductions for many years. When talking with parents during investigations, they all acknowledged that they could have likely done more to protect their children from the monsters who had changed their lives forever. We hope that the lessons in this book eliminate the chance of this happening to your family.

We also want to acknowledge that there is always a balance between safety and convenience. We have all seen "helicopter parents" who constantly watch over their children and prohibit any activity that may cause them any harm. While we possess a strong stance that parents should take action to create a private and secure world for their children, we know that an imaginary line exists between appropriate protection and overzealous guarding. Some parents hope their children make the right choices and release them into the world, while hoping for the best. Other parents block their children from Internet use and refuse to give them a cellular phone. We only hope that this book provides the information you need to identify the correct balance for your family.

Warning Signs

When it comes to kids and technology, there are often warning signs that they may be in trouble. Throughout this book we will educate you so that you are better equipped to recognize these warning signs and provide you with the information you need to take the proper steps to intervene, including strategic communication guidelines. Remember, it is never too late to start investing time and energy to keep your kids safe in the digital world.

At a young age, the most important move you can make is to ensure that your child is supervised when going online. This is entirely possible with your preschooler and, to some extent, with your preteen. When you start to assume this role of technology advisor at home, something we dive into later in the Parent Patrol chapter, your child will understand that you are wholeheartedly invested in their relationship with technology.

For younger kids, insist that your children use smartphones, tablets, or computers in either your kitchen or your living room (the most "public" gathering places in your house). This can help you stay up-to-date in terms of what your son or daughter is doing. While we often give children technology to give us a break, take two minutes before they start their Internet time to ask them what they plan to do and review the rules. The worst thing you can do is to ignore your children and assume they are making good decisions. Parents invest time guiding kids in many other areas of their lives from what they eat, to what they buy, to whom they friend. As soon as you allow a child to take technology into a private room, such as the bedroom, you are missing an opportunity to set boundaries. However, we recognize this is a difficult proposition as your child reaches the teen years, as this is no longer something you can entirely control.

The warning signs at all age levels most often include a change in behavior. Let's take a preschooler, for example. If your 5-year-old son loved going to the park, but is now glued to his iPad every waking second fighting zombies in Minecraft, it's time to intervene. Most importantly, this preschooler stage is where you need to teach good technology habits.

"Young children are very teachable and willing to learn and apply rules of conduct," explains Alyson Schafer, parenting expert and author of *Honey, I Wrecked the Kids*. "If you start training them how to behave online when they are young, they are more likely to respect those social rules. These habits will be deeply engrained by the time they hit the teen years."

With preteens, the hands-on work gets more intense. In some cases, this is also where you will have to start to concern yourself with physical security. Although for many parents this prompts conversations about strangers online, there are also other potential dangers.

Just recently, 11-year-old Davorius Gray from South Carolina died after accepting an Internet challenge. The deadly game, called "Hangman," encourages players to choke themselves until they pass out. This Internet craze, which is viral today, will be replaced with another dangerous stunt in the months to come. Being aware of the rising popularity of these dangerous challenges will equip you to have important conversations with your children. Davorius' mother, Latrice Hurst, said this to WYFF4 (her local news station), warning parents about the importance of staying engaged.

"If I could rewind time, I would go back and heavily monitor his use of social media, YouTube, and the Internet," Latrice said. "I would just say, I don't believe young people should be on social media and it should be limited to adults, or at the very least, with extreme adult supervision–where the parents can see everything that takes place on the sites–should be a requirement."

With teens, dangerous online situations are even more prevalent. Your children might start to get careless about what they share online–posting sexually explicit photos or bullying close friends in comments–blocking you from seeing any of their accounts. These actions don't always mean your children are in trouble, but you should monitor what they are doing to ensure that you aren't caught off guard if things escalate. "A healthy teen functioning properly should be able to keep up all their responsibilities," explains Schafer.

"Remember, they are preparing for adulthood, and as 'adults in training' they need to be ready to launch into a world without parental supervision. That means we need to educate and allow them an opportunity for more self-directed and self-disciplined behavior each year. But if your teen is evading or failing to maintain these responsibilities, parents need to discuss their concerns and step in if their teen can't manage to rectify their situation on their own." Schafer explains that these are some of the warning signs:

- Isolation from the family
- A drop in school performance
- Late night online activities
- Excessive gaming (gaming addictions are possible)
- Difficulties respecting no-phone/tech times (like the dinner table, church or movie theatre)
- Anxiety when they can't connect, or panic if they leave their phone at home
- Compulsive checking of devices (measured by minutes, not hours)
- Mood swings from elation to depression depending on their online social events
- Stress symptoms and/or sleep disturbance resulting from never getting "downtime"
- Physical complaints from repetitive strain or postural issues
- Loss of interest in their old offline recreational activities or hobbies

To add to this, we used to live in a world where the average teenager had a dozen or so close friends, but today this individual is easily connected to hundreds of people at their school, in their city, and well beyond. Their desire to collect friends (and likes!) online means that their definition of friendship is entirely different than the generation before them. As we talk about monitoring strategies for all social media networks later in the book, we will also discuss how to speak about these issues with your children. This will include the best way to approach these difficult conversations.

A Question from a Parent

Gill Livingston: My child now uses a Google Chromebook at school and uses Google Classroom and Google Drive. They're doing lots of online research for projects now. How can parents and school leaders ensure these tools are safe?

Amber's Answer: I hear this question at almost every presentation I give. Overall, most students using Google Chromebooks and Google's online services are protected. Google actually has some of the best online security in place that I have seen. The concern is how the data is managed internally at the school. Smart system administrators will be fairly "hands-off" and allow Google to protect the content. However, I have seen many school officials that alter security settings in a way that makes the data public over the Internet. While rare, it does happen. I always offer parents a simple search that can set their minds at ease. Use Michael's online search tool, explained in Chapter Ten, to search for your child's school name plus the words "Google," "Docs," and "Drive." In other words, conduct the following three searches within this tool across each option, including the quotation marks. If you discover any sensitive data, inform the school.

"Unionville High School" "Google"
"Unionville High School" "Docs"
"Unionville High School" "Drive"

Chapter Two
Facebook Concerns

If there is one social network that reaches across generations, it's Facebook. Although teens often boast about leaving Mark Zuckerberg's baby for trendier tech, Pew Research reported that, as of 2015, 71 percent of kids ages 13 to 17 use the site. Worldwide, Facebook has more than 1 billion daily active users. With such spectacular growth there are also spectacular privacy and safety challenges–challenges that affect us on an ongoing basis.

Since its launch in 2004, Facebook has matured as the online destination to share who we are dating, what we are liking, and where we are going. In its early years, it was increasingly difficult to delete your account once you were up and running, gradually stressing Facebook's relationship with its community. In 2010, they finally made it easier to sign off for good, but up until this point you had to remove each individual post by hand and hope that Facebook would answer your email requests to disconnect entirely. Nonetheless, this same year, the company hit a massive tipping point, boasting a whopping 500 million users.

Facebook Places also launched in the summer of 2010. This is the feature that "allows you to see where your friends are and share your location in the real world." As Facebook explains, "when you use Places, you'll be able to see if any of your friends are currently checked in nearby and connect with them easily." During this time, we heard many stories about friends checking friends into places they had never been, such as strip clubs and other incriminating locations. It was also during this time that Facebook slowly trained us to learn that if we want to better manage our privacy, we had to (in many cumbersome steps) opt out of these features as the company was definitely defaulting to opting us in.

In the coming years, the list of new features brought with them new privacy and safety issues. When Facebook bought Instagram, for example, they released a new Terms of Service agreement that gave the company permission to use your photos from either platform in ads without informing you. The next year, Graph Search made it easy to snoop on anyone. As *Gizmodo* explains in reference to Graph Search in the summer of 2013, "...in the wrong hands, it can be the ultimate stalker search engine." This post included a sentence commonly seen in how-to articles about Facebook privacy, "Here are the settings you need to adjust today to keep the Facebook creepers away." Again, it is always a user's responsibility to change settings so private information isn't public, although we accurately assume it should be the other way around.

What we forget is the money behind it all. Facebook collects our data because it needs to continue to fuel its advertising platform, making the company relevant and powerful for companies interested in targeting specific individuals with specific interests. The more they know, the more they make. Facebook's 2015 revenue was $17.93 billion. Yes, our data is big business. While more adults are now understanding that sharing has its dark side, too many children are sharing without any regard for their overall privacy and safety.

In this chapter, we'll discuss basic Facebook terminology, search strategies, profile extraction, and some easy hacks. Aside from these hard skills, parents must also learn the soft skills. In other words, it's essential to be creative about having conversations with our kids about what exactly they're doing on Facebook. Being creative doesn't mean throwing up our hands and loudly cursing Mark Zuckerberg at the dinner table, but instead it means seeing a little light through the door crack.

Here's how one British Columbia mom saw an opportunity to connect with her teenage kids on Facebook. While she desperately wanted to be a legitimate friend, she understood that it would be uncool to ask them to allow her into their treasured social network. Instead of forcing the issue, she came up with an original idea to further understand their Facebook lives.

As one of the neighborhood's most social families, she knew that everyone who came over to the house loved the family's dog, Marley. She decided to set up an account as the beloved pet. Not only did her children flock to the account, but their friends couldn't get enough of Marley's daily canine adventures. This allowed this mother to keep a close eye on communication in her kids' community. While this is against Facebook's official policies (a pet cannot have a personal account but can have a public page), this mom kept Marley's updates going strong for years to engage his many new teenage fans.

Facebook Terminology

Before talking about other hacks and strategies, let's look at some common Facebook terminology so you can stay in the loop on the latest lingo. Facebook has a lengthy glossary of terms on its website that is updated on a regular basis. Many of these are self-explanatory, but for parents who are relatively new to the Facebook universe, here are ten top terms that we will address on a regular basis.

Account settings: This is where you can manage all of your account preferences. Within your settings, which are in the top right side of your Facebook account, you can do the following:

- Learn how to permanently delete your account.
- Update name, email address, security settings, and privacy settings.
- Edit basic information on your profile.

Activity log: This view, which is only available to you as a user, is the tool that allows you to see and manage what you share.

Cover photo: This is the large photo on the top of your Facebook account. Your profile photo is the smaller square photo that appears on your account, but also appears when you post on someone else's account.

News feed: This is the heart of all Facebook activity. Within your news feed you will see updates from people, pages, and groups you follow. These updates do not appear in chronological order, but instead they depend on how much you interact with other accounts.

Tagging: Tagging is a common term used on Facebook (and other social media accounts) to link a person, page, or place to a post. Users most often use tags to include people in pictures they share.

Tag review: Within your settings, you can choose to review tags to control when a user includes you in a post. In other words, you can approve or dismiss a tag if you have this setting enabled.

Notes: This feature is Facebook's answer to blog posts. If you do turn on this feature, people will be able to see Notes in your profile.

Block: If someone is a bother to you, it's easy to block them on Facebook (they will not be notified). You can do this in two ways: block a person with their name and email address (click on the lock icon in top right corner), or go to the person's profile and click on the three horizontal dots on their cover photo.

Follow: If you are not friends with someone, you can still follow their updates if they have this feature enabled. You can think of this feature like a subscribe button so you get their updates in your news feed.

Groups: These are digital spaces on Facebook that allow you to have private conversations that do not show up in a news feed. Most often, you would use these to communicate with teammates or colleagues.

While the above gives you a formal introduction to official Facebook terminology, there are dozens of slang terms that people (especially kids!) use to communicate on Facebook (in news feeds, comments, Messenger, etc.).

Top 10 Facebook Slang Terms Parents Need to Know

Facebook is taking the slang business so seriously that it recently filed a patent to scan posts in an attempt to identify made-up terms and phrases that are rising in popularity. The company wants to own this social glossary so that it has a better understanding of terms that are bubbling up. While the slang terms below are popular on Facebook, they are also seen on other social media sites and within messaging apps.

IDEK: I don't even know
Bae: A term of endearment to describe someone
Netflix and chill: It's a term used for hooking up
GOAT: Greatest of all time
GNOC: Get naked on camera
ASL: Age, sex, location
CD9: Parents are around
IWSN: I want sex now
KPC: Keep parents clueless
PAW: Parents are watching

The previous list is just a small sample. Not only are there hundreds more, but there are new slang terms growing in popularity every month. As parents become aware of these slang terms, children tend to create and adopt new terminology.

How do I locate my child's Facebook profile?

Several years ago, searching your child's first and last name within the search field of any Facebook page would have likely presented a full profile ready for exploration. This would have included photos, timeline content, and many personal details such as interests and online activity. While some parents get lucky providing only a child's name to Facebook's search, most will receive irrelevant or partial results. Many children manipulate their profile data in order to stay hidden among the millions of random profiles. Some may alter the spelling of their name to hide from parents while others will use misleading screen names or completely false details. Regardless of your child's behavior, it is important to consider these possibilities. Also, rest assured that we will show you how to find practically any profile.

Before assuming your child is hiding inappropriate content from you, consider the possibility that he or she is hiding from a dangerous element. Many smart children know about the predators that peruse the Internet looking for the next victim. Your tech-savvy child may be providing misleading details as a remedy to avoid the constant bombardment of unwanted messages from online creeps. We point this out to encourage parents to applaud their children who are thinking a step ahead of this very bad element.

Parents may also want to consider the potential for a child to possess multiple profiles. Many kids will maintain a very overt Facebook profile containing innocent details for the sole purpose of satisfying your urge to snoop. Parents often monitor this bait and abandon further searches for the secondary profile that contains more revealing information about the child. We encourage parents to never stop searching for new profiles that have been created by your children. These "hidden" pages will likely reveal potential problems before the "public" accounts. The following content applies to every Facebook search situation.

Overall, Facebook users tend to keep their information a little more secure than users of other social networking sites. By default, a new Facebook user must specify the privacy settings to their account during the creation of their profile. This is mostly thanks to privacy advocates who continuously protest Facebook's privacy policies. Many of these user settings simply do not promote privacy and leave your child's information exposed for anyone to see. This section will explain numerous ways parents can obtain your child's Facebook information that is not visible on the public profile. Please note that you must be logged into an active Facebook account for the following methods to be effective. Some of these techniques may appear complicated at first; however, a robust online free search tool is presented at the end that will make the entire process painless.

Once logged in, a simple search field will be present at the top of any Facebook page. Typing in your child's real name should lead to some results. Unlike Twitter, Facebook users usually use their real name when creating a profile. This profile is also usually linked to an employer and school. Once your child's profile is located, the default view is the "timeline" tab. This will include basic information such as gender, location, family members, friends, relationship status, interests, education, and work background. This page will also commonly have a photo of your child and any recent posts on their page. With over a billion active users, it will be likely that you will locate several user profiles under the same name as your child. There are a few things that you can do to find the right profile.

If your child's name is Tom Johnson, you have your work cut out for you. This does not mean that you will never find his Facebook page, but you will need to take additional steps to get to him. When searching the name, several possibilities will appear in a drop-down menu. This is obviously not the complete list of Tom Johnsons who are present on Facebook. At the bottom of this list is an option to see all of the profiles with your child's name. After scrolling down through this list, you can select "See more results" to continue loading profiles with your child's name. You can look through these and hope to identify your target based on the photo, location, or additional information displayed in this view. Unfortunately, you may not see your child's profile in these results. You will likely receive better search results by using a custom website address. The following URL (website address) would identify any profiles with the name of Tom Johnson.

www.facebook.com/search/str/Tom Johnson/users-named

This is a much more direct way of submitting the name of Tom Johnson to Facebook's servers. The result will contain two advantages. First, it will bypass the general search result window that includes recommended accounts, such as celebrities. Next, it will display every profile of individuals on Facebook with the supplied name. At the time of this writing, you can achieve the same results by typing People named "Tom Johnson" in the Facebook search field. Regardless of which option you choose, this method will provide more thorough and accurate results.

Facebook can also help you find current and past employees of a business. This can be beneficial if you cannot locate your child's profile and he or she is employed. Young adults often share their employment status on their profiles as a way to convey maturity. If your child works at a local coffee shop called "Bancroft's," the following website address would provide the best results.

www.facebook.com/search/str/bancrofts/pages-named/employees/present

Changing "present" to "past" within this address will identify profiles of people who are likely no longer employed by the company. If your child worked at Bancroft's in the past, and likely provided that detail on his or her profile, the following address would probably identify the profile.

www.facebook.com/search/str/bancrofts/pages-named/employees/past

You can also combine search options into one query. If you wanted to search for all Bancroft's employees named "Tom Johnson," the following exact queries into any Facebook page would produce results.

People named "Tom Johnson" who work at Bancroft's
People named "Tom Johnson" who worked at Bancroft's

Facebook also allows you to filter search results by a topic of interest. When your child clicks the "like" button on a Facebook page, the profiles can be searched by this data. The exact address to view every Facebook user who likes coffee would be as follows.

www.facebook.com/search/str/coffee/pages-named/likers

You could also search "people who like coffee" within the Facebook search bar and receive very similar results. This can be very beneficial if you know a handful of musical groups that your child likes. If your child likes the band Thrice and attends Harvard, the following precise website would likely include a link to that child's profile.

www.facebook.com/search/str/Harvard/pages-named/students/str/Thrice/pages- named/likers/intersect

We have experienced mixed results when searching for this content within the Facebook search pane. The above example could likely be replicated by searching "People who like Thrice and attend Harvard." Obviously, you would replace these examples with content relevant to your child. As a worst-case scenario, Facebook allows you to search for all students of a specific school without knowing names. This can be beneficial for locating your child's profile when an alias name or misspelled name is used on the page. The following search would identify every current and past student of Harvard University.

www.facebook.com/search/str/harvard/pages-named/students

If your child attends a school with small enrollment, this method should work well. We see parents use this technique to quickly view a list of every student at the school. Within moments of scrolling, they find a photo of their child next to an alias name. This success often indicates that much more revealing information about the child is about to be exposed.

Facebook has another useful search feature. You can enter an email address and it will identify any profile that was created using that email address. In most scenarios, you can provide this address in the main search field on any Facebook page. Simply type the exact email address of your child, including the domain such as gmail.com or yahoo.com, and you will be presented the profile that is associated with the account. This is a great way to identify Facebook profiles created by your child regardless of the name provided. Some children have taken steps to prevent this type of discovery; however, there is another solution. Submit the search as a website address, or URL. The following website address will identify any Facebook profiles that were registered to the email address tom.smith@gmail.com.

www.facebook.com/search/results.php?q=tom.smith@gmail.com

This will link to the profile and provide the basic information associated with the account. This is also beneficial when trying to locate a child who has an unknown nickname instead of a real name on their profile. We believe that you should conduct these searches providing every known email address your child has ever used. Many parents ask their children for their Facebook profile addresses and are met with resistance or deceit. Those same parents that ask for the children's email addresses are often met with compliance. This is a great way to locate Facebook profiles without disclosing the action to a child. Most children have no knowledge of these techniques.

If you have struck-out identifying your child's Facebook profile with the previous searches, there is one last technique that is very effective. The vast majority of Facebook profiles are associated with a cellular telephone number. When your child created a Facebook account, he or she was likely asked to provide an active telephone number in order to verify identity. Children provide this information without much thought. When they do, they connect the provided number with the account. If a child installs the Facebook app on a mobile device, the associated number is shared with Facebook. While this may seem intrusive, it can be a benefit to parents. You can search by your child's telephone number and locate any associated profiles. There is a Facebook website that allows you to reset your password if you have forgotten it. You must be completely logged out of Facebook before visiting this page, which can be located at the following address.

https://www.facebook.com/login/identify?ctx=recover

This will present a single search field that will accept an email address, a telephone number, a user name, or a real name. If you enter any of this information about your child, you should receive a result identifying the profile with the full name used. This essentially provides the world's greatest cellular telephone number search engine. The information provided may identify other partial email addresses and will confirm the last two digits of all telephone numbers attached to the account. Do not click "Continue" on this screen, as it will send a password reset request to your child. This would not lock him or her out of the account or gain you access, but it could raise suspicion. This search will display the name that your child is using on the account and the profile photo visible during a search by that name. This image can help identify the appropriate profile when you search directly on Facebook with the name provided to Facebook by your child.

What if my child has a "Private" account?

At this point, you should be able to locate your child's profile and analyze the publicly available content by scrolling through the pages. That is just the tip of the iceberg. Facebook collects a lot of additional information from everyone's activity on the social network. Every time your child "Likes" something or is tagged in a photo, Facebook stores that information. Until recently, this was sometimes difficult to locate, if not impossible. You will not always find these "hidden" details on your child's profile page, but the new Facebook Graph search allows us to dig into this information.

In order to conduct the following detailed searches, you must know the user number of your child's Facebook account. This number is a unique identifier that will allow us to search otherwise hidden information from Facebook. The first option involves viewing the source code of your child's Facebook profile within a web browser, and is quite cumbersome. Instead, this is a good time to introduce a custom search page created to simplify this process for parents. Navigate to the following website, which will be referenced throughout the remainder of this section.

www.inteltechniques.com/osint/facebook.html

The top left portion of this page displays a small search field titled "Facebook User Name" followed by "Displays User Number." If you enter your child's Facebook user name here, the tool will fetch their user number for the next searches. Before you can use this tool to obtain details about your child's activity, you must identify their Facebook user name. User names are very different than real names provided by your child. User names are often created by Facebook without input from the child. They may be michael.bazzell.7 or amber.mac.62. Your child's user name will always be visible in the website address when you are looking at their Facebook profile. Below are two examples of Facebook profile addresses.

www.facebook.com/michael.bazzell.7?fref=nf
www.facebook.com/amber.mac.62/friends

In each of these examples, there is data before and after the user name. You must be able to identify and isolate only the user name from within this address. The easiest way is to always view the home page of your child's Facebook profile. The user name begins immediately after facebook.com/.

The user name ends before any question mark (?) or forward slash (/). In the above examples, the user names are michael.bazzell.7 and amber.mac.62. You can now place your child's user name into the search tool mentioned previously and identify the user number of your child's Facebook account. The figure on page 29 displays this feature. The example used the Facebook user name of TonyRobbins which revealed the associated user number of 111783969059.

In some rare scenarios, your child may not have a Facebook user name, often referred to as a vanity name. If this is the case, you will see the entire Facebook user number within the website address of your child's profile. It may appear similar to facebook.com/651620441. In this example, 651620441 is your child's user number. We will use this number for numerous searches within the next instruction. You can test your understanding of the following methods using this number, and should receive live results.

Up to this point, we have made quite a fuss about obtaining your child's user number on Facebook. This step is vital in order to unlock the vast data that is often hidden from your view. You will only need to do this once, as the number never changes, unless your child creates a new account. The following information may appear very technical and out of reach to those who avoid complex technology. However, we promise that the free online tools will make all of this easy. The idea here is that much of your child's activity is not visible on his or her public profile. Children can choose to remove categories of details such as likes, events, or videos from their profiles. Parents visit a child's profile and see nothing since kids often "remove" this content. When a child chooses to eliminate content from public view, it does not make it "private." Most children believe that only their friends can see sensitive details because they cannot see it themselves when logged out of their account. This is very misleading, as you will see next.

Let's start with something basic. Assume that your child's profile does not display his or her likes. You cannot see all of the places, pages, objects, and celebrities in which your child possesses an interest. The following two website addresses make all of this reappear. Replace the included user number with that which was assigned to your child.

www.facebook.com/search/651620441/places-liked
www.facebook.com/search/651620441/pages-liked

The first link displays every place, such as a business or school that your child has "liked." The second displays every Facebook profile, regardless of type, that your child has "liked." This information can be very revealing. Parents who discover musical groups, teen celebrities, and innocent products can rest a bit knowing their child is behaving similar to most adolescents. However, the parent that sees signs of drug usage, alcohol abuse, or other inappropriate activities can strategize a long talk. If you want to see any photos on Facebook that your child has "liked," you can type the following address into a web browser.

www.facebook.com/search/651620441/photos-liked

This basic structure contains the website (facebook.com), the action (search), the user number (651620441), and the requested information (photos-liked). Since these are photos that were "liked" by your child, the results will include photos on other people's pages that would have been difficult to locate otherwise. If you had asked Facebook for this information with only the name of your child, you would have been denied. If your child has a common name, a name search would not work. The method described here works because we know your child's user number. There are many other options with this search.

This technique can be used to locate additional photos of your child, the apps he or she is using on a smartphone, hidden videos from a profile, and the events being held to which your child has received an invitation. We are about to demonstrate the many ways to conduct advanced searches within Facebook that are not well known. We ask you to use responsibility while performing your searches. Consider limiting the profiles searched only to those of your family members. While none of our methods are illegal or unethical, these actions might seem intrusive to others. Please use your best judgment.

Michael's Hacks

You can navigate to the following addresses to see more information about your child (example user number 651620441). You may be surprised at the amount of visible content that your child likely assumes is "private." Explanations of each address will be explained after the list. You should replace 651620441 with the user ID of your child. Please note that the remaining Facebook techniques will only function if your Facebook profile language settings are set to English (US). Any other languages will produce an error. The following links are included in order to provide a "behind the scenes" look at what is going on. The search tool disclosed after these details simplifies this technique, and makes the following sections optional reading.

www.facebook.com/search/651620441/places-visited
www.facebook.com/search/651620441/recent-places-visited
www.facebook.com/search/651620441/places-checked-in
www.facebook.com/search/651620441/places-liked
www.facebook.com/search/651620441/pages-liked
www.facebook.com/search/651620441/photos-by
www.facebook.com/search/651620441/photos-liked
www.facebook.com/search/651620441/photos-of
www.facebook.com/search/651620441/photos-commented
www.facebook.com/search/651620441/videos
www.facebook.com/search/651620441/videos-by
www.facebook.com/search/651620441/videos-of
www.facebook.com/search/651620441/videos-liked
www.facebook.com/search/651620441/videos-commented
www.facebook.com/search/651620441/apps-used
www.facebook.com/search/651620441/friends
www.facebook.com/search/651620441/events
www.facebook.com/search/651620441/events-joined
www.facebook.com/search/651620441/stories-by
www.facebook.com/search/651620441/stories-commented
www.facebook.com/search/651620441/stories-tagged
www.facebook.com/search/651620441/groups
www.facebook.com/search/651620441/relatives

The "places-visited" option will display locations that your child has physically visited and allowed Facebook to collect the location information. This is often completed through a smartphone, sometimes unintentionally.

The "recent-places-visited" option will display locations that your child has recently physically visited if they allowed Facebook to collect their location information. This feature is not always reliable, and a definitive time frame of "recent" has not been established.

The "places-checked-in" option will display locations where your child has used the Facebook app to "check in." While this can be falsified, these results are usually more accurate and believable than "places-visited."

The "places-liked" option will display any physical locations that your child has clicked "like." This will often identify favorite clubs and special restaurants. This can be priceless information for a parent trying to locate a child past curfew or a runaway while missing.

The "pages-liked" option will display any Facebook pages that your child liked. This will often display interests of your child such as a favorite sports team, musical group, or television show. These results will include a button labeled "liked by." Clicking this will identify everyone on Facebook who liked that item. This can quickly identify the people who also like a local trouble spot about which you are concerned.

The "photos-by" option will display Facebook photos that were uploaded by your child. These will likely already be visible on your child's photos page. However, this search could potentially reveal additional images.

The "photos-liked" option was explained on the previous page. This can be beneficial if your child has a private profile. If the photos of interest are on someone else's profile that is not private, you will be able to see all of them.

The "photos-of" option will display any photos in which your child has been tagged. This will immediately locate additional photos of your child that may not be visible on your child's profile. This is helpful when the photos are private on one person's page, but not others. This is often the most used search by parents.

The "photos-commented" option will display any photos on profiles where your child left a comment on the photo. This can be important because your child may not have "liked" the photo nor been tagged in it. The option may produce redundant results, but it should always be checked.

The "videos" option will display videos visible on your child's profile. These may or may not be directly connected to your child. They could also be videos linked to the original source with no personal ties to your child. Many children choose to eliminate videos from their profiles.

The "videos-by" option will display videos that were actually uploaded by your child. These will be much more personal to your child and will usually include more relevant content. This method will often display videos associated with your child that are not viewable on their public profile.

The "videos-of" option is similar to the "photos-of" filter. This will display videos that supposedly contain images of your child within the video itself. It could be compared to "tagging" someone inside a video. These will likely include videos of your child stored on other children's Facebook accounts.

The "videos-liked" option will display any videos that your child clicked "like". This can also be used to establish personal interests of the child and are often of interest to parents.

The "videos-commented" option will display any videos on profiles where your child left a comment on the video. Again, this can be important because your child may not have "liked" the video nor been tagged in it. The option may produce redundant results, but it should always be checked.

The "apps-used" option will display any apps installed through Facebook. These are usually games that can be played with other people, and may identify the latest craze that keeps your child glued to the device.

The "friends" option should display a list of all of your child's friends on Facebook. This will be the same list visible on the main profile page. If you receive no results, your child likely has the friends list set to "private."

The "events" option will display any Facebook events that your child was invited to attend. These often include parties, company events, concerts, and other social gatherings. This will usually display events that are not listed on the child's profile, as these are hidden by default.

The "events-joined" option will only display the Facebook events that your child acknowledged attendance. This could be in the form of an "R.S.V.P." or confirmation by the child that he or she is currently at the event. This could be used to confirm that your child was present at the under-age drinking party that you read about in the newspaper.

The "stories-by" option will display any public posts by your child. This can often identify posts that are not currently visible on your child's profile. The results provided are never complete, and many hidden posts may still exist. The goal with this method is to identify whether your child is deliberately hiding some posts and not others.

The "stories-commented" option will display any public posts by any users if your child entered a comment. This is useful in identifying communication from your child with a private profile. The standard privacy options do not prevent a search of your comment history on public posts.

The "stories-tagged" option will display any posts in which your child was tagged. This tagging is usually performed because of an interest in the post. This will likely identify posts from other children who are associated with your child. This method usually identifies friends of your child who might not be listed within the profile's "Friends" list.

The "groups" option will display any groups of which your child is a member. This is beneficial in identifying stronger interests of your child. In my experience, a child must only have faint interest to "like" something. However, the interest is usually strong if a group related to the topic is joined by the child. This can identify involvement with inappropriate groups related to drugs, sex, or violence.

The "relatives" option will display a list of people who your child has identified as a relative. Often, this will display relatives even if your child has the friends list set to "private."

Facebook Search Tool

You may now be wondering how you are going to implement all of these searches in an easy format. We had the same thought and developed our own web tools to handle this task at the following website.

inteltechniques.com/osint/facebook.html

Navigate to this website in order to access an all-in-one solution. This is the same page that was referenced earlier while explaining advanced profile search options. The entire left side of this page will allow you to conduct all of the Facebook Graph searches that were mentioned in this section. The current state of this tool is visible on page 29.

The first group of searches allow you to attempt to locate your child's profile by email address or cellular number. A more reliable way to search by cellular number was explained earlier. The next option displays the profile ID number (user number) for your child's profile when providing the user name. Immediately below that is a field to enter your child's user number and submit in order to populate this number within the remaining search fields. This is useful when executing all possible searches quickly. The following section displays the individual "liked," "tagged," "event," and "by" information that was previously discussed.

The entire right half of this search page is focused toward Facebook searches outside of an individual profile. It allows you to search by name, location, employer, and other filters previously mentioned. It identifies the type of search within each search box. As an example, typing "Microsoft" in the third search option would immediately display any profiles that previously announced employment at Microsoft. The lower options allow you to combine searches. Entering "Drugs" and "Microsoft" in the "People who like... and worked at..." option would display profiles of former Microsoft employees who clicked "Like" on the Drugs Facebook page. Overall, this tool is not doing anything that you could not do on your own using the methods previously mentioned. Its purpose is to make searching easier. The Multiple Variables option near the bottom will allow you to select multiple filters and launch the appropriate search. You can choose as many or as few of the following options you wish to generate your own custom search. Clicking "And" after each input will present an additional search field.

Name	Language Spoken School
Current Employer or Title	Affiliation Places
Previous Employer or Title	Visited Pages
Current Home Location	Liked
Previous Home Location	Year Born

With this tool, you could quickly find your child's Facebook profile by knowing just a few generic pieces of data. Assume that your son's name is Tom Johnson, and you are having a hard time finding his profile. You know that he likes the band Billy Talent, and that he lives in Alton, Illinois. You suspect that he has mentioned that he currently works at Starbucks. You could use the multiple variables tool in the following manner.

Accept the default "Name" entry and insert Tom Johnson. Click the "And" button and choose the drop-down option of "Current Home Address." Enter "Alton" and click the "And" button. Choose the drop-down option of "Liked" and insert Billy Talent. Click "And" and choose the option of "Current Employer or Title." Insert Starbucks and click "Search." The result will be a page displaying every profile that belongs to someone named Tom Johnson, lives in a city called Alton, works at a Starbucks, and likes the band Billy Talent.

We recommend using this tool with minimal identifiers at first. The above example would likely produce no results as it is too specific. There is likely no one profile that fits the criteria. Instead, begin with two identifiers and progress as needed. Most parents only need to enter three pieces of data in order to filter the results from millions of Facebook profiles to only a few that match the search. Your results will vary, and this method takes practice.

Summary

As we mentioned at the beginning of this chapter, if your child is active on one social networking site, Facebook is probably it. In many ways, Zuckerberg's baby is the ultimate all-service platform. They've worked hard to be all things to all users—from a photo platform for families, to a live video platform for broadcasters, to an ad platform for marketers, to a messaging platform for friends. Other companies are starting to follow suit, or in some cases, play catch-up.

For example, Snapchat is working hard to peck away at Facebook's dominance in a couple of areas. Their messaging functionality is now much more sophisticated, including video and audio chat capabilities, video and audio notes, and stickers. This takes their business well beyond its initial launch as a photo-sharing site (or as many parents called it, a sexting service). Snapchat and Facebook are also neck and neck when it comes to daily video views. Plus, you're now commonly seeing both companies launch similar features or acquire apps in a race to be first to market with their youngest fans.

One thing we have not yet addressed in the context of Facebook is the gender split among teens. As Pew Research Center reported in its Teens, Social Media & Technology Overview 2015, 45 percent of boys said they used Facebook vs 36 percent of girls. Turns out that girls are opting for more visual tools, such as Instagram and Tumblr. One of the reasons girls tend to be heavy users of these platforms is that they are, statistically, more frequent sharers when it comes to photos and images; boys, on the other hand, outpace girls when it comes to time playing video games on consoles, online, and on phones.

After using the tools we've outlined above and digesting the information about how your son or daughter is commonly using Facebook, you're probably wondering what's next. Within the next four chapters we'll show you more ways, tools, and hacks to outsmart your kids online on today's most popular sites and within today's most popular apps. Once you're more familiar with today's fast-paced digital landscape, we will provide best practices to manage everything from screen time to targeted attacks to reporting issues. Again, we will also close the gap, so to speak, with expert advice on how to strategically start these conversations with your children and take action right now to keep them safe.

A Question from a Parent

Richard Gillespie: Luckily my kids aren't into chatting yet (10 and 4 years old), but once they are old enough that would be my main concern. Then there's the inevitable bullying that will occur. It seems kids are "afraid" of un-friending people who aren't real friends from how I've seen younger relatives behave on FB. And since they continue to stay friends with bullies, it only gets worse. And in many ways the verbal bullying online is worse than physical bullying in or around school. What should a parent do?

Amber's Answer: According to DoSomething.com, more than 3.2 million American students are victims of bullying every year. Even more disturbing, this same site says 1 in 4 teachers see nothing wrong with bullying and only intervene 4 percent of the time. One of the best resources online for both parents and teachers when it comes to bullying is TheBullyProject.com. This site includes a parent action toolkit to explain how to talk to your children, how to approach the school, and other next steps. While instinctively parents want to advise a child to block a bully online, the truth is that sometimes this can lead to further retaliation. The guide reinforces this unfortunate reality, "One of the reasons teenagers don't report bullying is humiliation. Older children report bullying less often than younger children because they are often embarrassed and fear retaliation." If you want to empower your children as they get older and will inevitably have to deal with bullies online, suggest they keep a good record or diary of what's happening. The more carefully this is documented, without notifying the bully, the better the chance for a positive intervention. We will further address bullying and best practices in Chapter 8: Targeted Attacks.

INTELTECHNIQUES.com

MICHAEL BAZZELL
OSINT TRAINER &
PRIVACY CONSULTANT

| Home | Blog | Forum | Online Training | Live Training | Bio | Privacy | Tools | Books | Contact |

Custom Facebook Tools

Search Target Profile:

Email Address	GO	(Account by Email)
Disabled for most users	GO	(Account by Cell Phone)
TonyRobbins	GO	(Displays User Number)

> 111783969059

| Facebook User Number | GO | (Populate All) |

Facebook User Number	GO	(Displays Places Visited)
Facebook User Number	GO	(Displays Recent Places Visited)
Facebook User Number	GO	(Displays Places Checked-In)
Facebook User Number	GO	(Displays Places Liked)
Facebook User Number	GO	(Displays Pages Liked)
Facebook User Number	GO	(Displays Photos By User)
Facebook User Number	GO	(Displays Photos Liked)
Facebook User Number	GO	(Displays Photos Of -Tagged)
Facebook User Number	GO	(Displays Photo Comments)
Facebook User Number	GO	(Displays Apps Used)
Facebook User Number	GO	(Displays Videos)
Facebook User Number	GO	(Displays Videos Of User)
Facebook User Number	GO	(Displays Videos By User)
Facebook User Number	GO	(Displays Videos Liked)
Facebook User Number	GO	(Displays Video Comments)
Facebook User Number	GO	(Displays Event Invitations)
Facebook User Number	GO	(Displays Events Attended)
Facebook User Number	GO	(Displays Posts by User)
Facebook User Number	GO	(Displays Post Comments)
Facebook User Number	GO	(Displays Posts Tagged)
Facebook User Number	GO	(Displays Groups)
Facebook User Number	GO	(Displays Co-Workers)
Facebook User Number	GO	(Displays Friends)
Facebook User Number	GO	(Displays Relatives)
Facebook User Number	GO	(Displays Friends' Likes)

| Facebook User Number | ALL | (Run all-Must allow pop-ups) |

Chapter Three
Twitter Concerns

#ViralInternetChallenges

In our first chapter we warned you about Internet challenges. Earlier in spring 2016, Twitter was ground zero for another digital dare. Although this fad wasn't excessively dangerous, there were a number of teens who suffered mild injuries. Just the name of this challenge demonstrates how even the silliest of ideas can go viral. After all, it is the story of a boy and a banana peel.

The #BananaPeelChallenge started with Jason Oakes, a kid who tweeted out that he wanted to see if this fruit skin was as slippery as it appeared to be in famous kids' cartoons. After sliding on the peel a couple of times, he falls backwards (presumably on his head) with his feet up in the air. The views came in past one hundred thousand, and so did the fans.

It would be nearly impossible to predict that something so bizarre would entice thousands of copycats around the world, yet this is exactly what happened. A quick search of "#BananaPeelChallenge" on Twitter (see more on searching below) will yield some pretty entertaining, but equally painful, videos.

140 Characters Turns Deadly

On a more serious note, like all social media platforms, there are plenty of examples of extreme bullying and harassment on Twitter. In some cases, even just a few short words can be fatal.

In February 2016, this headline, "Indy teen murdered because of comments made on Twitter" went viral. According to court documents, 18-year-old Jerrold Parker was shot, and later died in a hospital, after tweeting that a 19-year-old acquaintance and his friends couldn't rap.

While this is an extreme example, it does show the power of 140 characters. When a teen shames a peer in such a public online space, many times there are instances of rage–and unfortunately, revenge. Part of the power of

Twitter is its plain interface and simple experience, but that also means it's often too easy to throw hurtful words in someone's face without thinking about the consequences.

Teen Twitter Lingo

In the spring of 2015, Pew Internet Center found that 33 percent of American teens use Twitter. The biggest users among teens were boys and girls ages 15 to 17. Similar to Facebook, we often hear about the dramatic fall of Twitter. Endless headlines claim that young people do not use this service, but time and again we discover that the opposite is true. While new user growth among this age group may not be increasing in a significant manner, 33 percent of teens is still a significant number. Like all things digital, teens have created their very own Twitter rules of engagement, as danah boyd, researcher and author of *It's Complicated: The Social Lives of Networked Teens*, says to *Fast Company* in reference to teens on Twitter.

"The first thing you would notice if you were following teenagers is that you would not see very many links. Which is radically different than our world. They're doing a lot of interacting and engaging around celebrities, pop culture, really funny trending topics that they think are interesting."

Microsoft was recently so intrigued to understand how young people engage in 140 characters or less that it launched "Tay," a chatbot that uses artificial intelligence to try to tweet like a teen. Within its first few days online, someone overtook the bot and programmed it to send out sexually explicit and racially insensitive messages. Plus, the bot got caught "talking" about smoking marijuana (kush) in the wrong company with this little tweet:

"kush! [I'm smoking kush infront the police]"

Microsoft quickly shut down the experiment and set Tay's account to private. Heck, if only parents could reset their kids when they make mistakes on Twitter and start over that easily. Instead, it's all about learning how this tiny tool works.

Twitter 101 for Parents

For parents, Twitter is a great platform for staying on top of breaking news, engaging in political conversations, and networking with colleagues. If you have a complaint about an airline or your cable company, Twitter is probably your fastest path to solid customer service. In a 2015 survey posted on the *American Press Institute* website, this is the breakdown of why people use Twitter.

To be alerted about breaking news
To keep up with the news in general
To pass the time
To tell others what I am thinking about
To see what people are talking about
To keep in touch with people I know
To follow famous people
To share news
To network
To follow trending topics

Not surprisingly, the majority of all users access Twitter on a smartphone (with teens, it's the vast majority). As for the company's breakthrough moment, it was on January 15, 2009 when the pilots of US Airways Flight 1549 glided their powerless plane on to the Hudson River. A few minutes later, Janis Krums tweeted a photo of the aircraft with its inflated rafts filled with passengers and captioned it with this message:

"There's a plane in the Hudson. I'm on the ferry going to pick up the people. Crazy."

Today that image has been viewed more than one million times.

While there are many reasons why Twitter is one of the more important social media utilities, as you can see from the stories at the top of this chapter, there are also many reasons why parents need to be empowered on this platform. Like other social networks, Twitter is rapidly expanding its reach into other verticals. While it started as a place to share what are essentially public text messages, it now allows users to upload photos and videos (oh, and let's not forget its popular GIFs). Plus, Twitter owns the famous Vine app, which lets users create short six-second videos.

Within this next section we will teach you everything you need to know to keep your kids safe on Twitter. Whether you want to find out if your daughter is sharing her location on Twitter, or if you need to do a deep dive to find your child's ongoing history of tweets, we will outline the tools below. If your child has deleted tweets, we can also give you some steps to dig them up on the Internet.

However, for starters, we will show you some basic search strategies. We will demonstrate how to find your child's Twitter profile–a task that often involves more legwork than locating your child on other platforms since Twitter does not require registered users to sign up with a real name. In fact, many teens prefer to use a unique handle that their parents might not find, unless you have our help. Before we dive into the best search strategies, you should be aware of the terminology you are likely to encounter on Twitter.

Top 10 Official Twitter Terms Parents Need to Know

As you learned when we reviewed Facebook terminology, most social networks share some sort of official glossary of terms online. Twitter is no exception, and perhaps they need it the most. Over the years, there have been a number of complaints from new Twitter users who struggle to learn how the company's unique symbols and language work. Here is a brief terminology guide.

@: The @ symbol is perhaps at the core of how Twitter works. This is how you communicate with fellow users. For example, to ensure that Twitter notices a message from you, you would write "Hello @Twitter, excited to learn more about how to communicate here." When someone includes your Twitter handle in a message, you will see it in the notifications section. In short, each user name should always include the @ symbol before it.

#: The # symbol is called the pound sign or number sign. On Twitter, it's how you group conversations. Every word (or phrase) that includes a # is called a hashtag. For example, if I want to write a funny tweet about parenting, I would write "This morning my child threw her Fruit Loops in my fresh coffee #MomProblems." If another user wants to read all of the tweets about "Mom Problems," she can simply use #MomProblems in her search to get started.

Follow: While having someone following you sounds like a creepy experience, if you want to build your Twitter following, it can be a good thing. This means someone is essentially subscribing to your feed on Twitter (using the "Follow" button), so this person is called a follower. To describe how many people are following you, this is your Follower Count. It is easy to follow someone, but equally as easy to choose to unfollow them.

Geolocation or geotagging: We later talk about the feature to search by location, but here is a teaser. This means that you essentially tag your tweet to tell people where you were when you wrote it. More and more, the next generation of social media users likes to tie his or her content to a location. This can be extremely problematic in terms of privacy and security.

Mention: A mention on Twitter is also the same as a reply. When someone mentions you they may not necessarily need you to reply to their message, but instead it simply indicates that they included you in their tweet. For example, they may say "We are going to @WaltDisneyWorld, cannot wait!" This doesn't necessarily mean that they need an answer or comment to this message, but instead it is simply a mention. Most individuals and brands do in fact reply to these mentions to engage in conversations. Depending on the age group, it is often considered rude if you don't respond to a mention (we will talk about this further in social media etiquette).

Parody: Although you understand what the word parody means in terms of spoofing something in a witty way, on Twitter it's worth noting that there are a number of parody accounts. Individuals will often create these handles (user names) to build a following on a popular (or trending) topic. In all cases, they are supposed to disclose that they are running a parody account (in their short bio on Twitter), but most do not follow this rule. As the company explains in its support section, impersonating someone is a different thing and is strictly prohibited. A good example of a Twitter parody account is @notzuckerberg. This feed pokes fun at Facebook's founder in a light and humorous way with tweets, such as "Any of you offering Black Friday deals on your personal data? Asking for a friend."

Pinned Tweet: For now, Twitter runs in reverse-chronological order so the newest tweets appear on the top of a user's feed. However, Twitter added a feature a while back to allow you to pin a tweet. This means that you can choose a tweet that you want to stay at the top of your Twitter account. Many users find pinned tweets confusing because they are so familiar with reading the latest tweets first, but a pinned tweet is always there. Many companies use this pinned tweet feature so you will see an ongoing promotion, or a teen may use this pinned tweet if they want to highlight a recent selfie with Justin Bieber.

Direct Messages: Direct messages are called DMs for short. A direct message is a private conversation with another Twitter user (also, you can also have private group DMs with multiple users). There have been a number of examples since Twitter's launch when a user thought they were sending a private message but instead it was shared publicly in that person's Twitter feed. If you search #DMfails on Twitter, you will see a number of these examples. Although it seems like an irresponsible thing to do, we want to stress again how easy it is to slip up and send a private message publicly on Twitter — especially if your teen, for example, is quickly messaging on their phone while doing a number of other tasks.

cc: Although this isn't an official Twitter term, it is commonly used on Twitter. To cc someone on Twitter refers to a carbon copy, similar to what you would do when you wanted to include a number of people in an email. Here's an example of how this would work. "Outsmarting Your Kids Online is a great book for any parent cc @ambermac @inteltechniques." In this example, the tweeter is sending the message to his or her friends, but wants to include us in a cc mention as the book's co-authors.

RT: An RT is a commonly used feature on Twitter. RT means Retweet, which means you are copying an exact message from another user and sharing it with your followers. Twitter also now makes it easy to RT something with your own personal comment attached. When you click the RT button, which looks like two bent arrows below a tweet, you can simply add a comment to this message. You will commonly see Twitter users say, in their profiles, that a RT does not equal endorsement. This means that they are simply sharing to highlight these messages, but again, it does not mean they agree with the content.

How do I search Twitter?

The Twitter search page located at **www.twitter.com/search-advanced** will help every parent begin their search for information relative to their child. This page will allow for the search of specific people, keywords, and locations. The problem here is that the search of a topic is often limited to the previous seven to ten days. Individual profiles should display tweets as far back as you are willing to scroll through. This can be a good place to search for recent data, but complete archives of a topic will not be displayed. You can conduct a search in the "This exact phrase" box to get precise results. Typing any words in the "None of these words" box will filter out any posts that include the chosen word or words. The "Hashtags" option will locate specific posts that mention a topic as defined by a Twitter hashtag. This is a single word preceded by a pound sign (#) that identifies a topic of interest. This allows users to follow certain topics without knowing user names of the user submitting the messages.

The "People" section allows you to search for tweets from a specific user. This can also be accomplished by typing the user name into the address bar after the Twitter domain. An example can be found at the website www.twitter.com/ambermac. This will display the user's profile including recent tweets.

The "To these accounts" field allows you to enter a specific Twitter user name. The results will only include tweets that were sent to the attention of the user. This can help identify associates of your child and information intended for him or her to read. Entering to:user name will replicate this option. If ambermac was your target, typing to:ambermac within any Twitter search field would give you the same result as entering the name in this advanced search option.

The "Places" field allows for the input of a zip code and selection of distance. The default 15 miles setting would produce tweets posted from within 15 miles of the perimeter of the zip code supplied. If using this option, we recommend choosing the 1 kilometer option, as it is the most constrictive radius that can be searched. In a moment, we will explain a more effective search technique for location.

The results of any of these searches can provide surprisingly personal information about your child. Much of the content may be useless banter. When a child declares that he was at a friend's house the entire weekend, but his Twitter feed displays his tweet about hanging out at the mall until midnight, he has some explaining to do. On several occasions, police officers have used this service to locate runaway children. Additionally, teenagers tend to brag about their activities on sites like Twitter, including vandalism, theft, and violence.

How do I find my child's Twitter profile?

Locating your child's Twitter profile may not be easy. Unlike Facebook and Google+, most Twitter users do not use their real name as their profile name. You need a place to search by real name. We recommend Twitter's "Who to follow" search page at **www.twitter.com/#!/who_to_follow**. Loading this page presents a single search option under the Twitter bar that can handle any real name. While scrolling down the list, you can look through the photo icons and brief descriptions to identify your child. Clicking on the user name will open the Twitter profile with more information.

Twitter's Who To Follow option can be great when you know the exact name that your child used when creating an account. If you are unsure of the real name provided, or if your child has a very common name, Followerwonk can help you identify the profile that you are seeking. This service, located at the website **www.followerwonk.com/bio,** allows you to search Twitter profiles for any keyword that may help you locate a profile of interest. You can choose the default "Profiles" search or the focused "Twitter Bios Only" option. The "More Options" under the main search box will display numerous fields including Location, Name, and Follower details. A search of "John Smith" reveals 21,156 Twitter profiles. However, a search of "John Smith" from "New York City" reveals only 81 profiles. Filtering out profiles that have not posted at least 100 tweets reveals only 31 profiles. This is a manageable number of profiles that can be viewed to identify your child.

If you still cannot locate your child's profile, you may need to resort to the Twitter Directory. This awkward and difficult monstrosity tries to allow you to browse through the millions of Twitter profiles alphabetically. First, choose the first letter of the first name of your child. This will present a range of options. You then need to select the range in which your child would be listed in, and that selection would open a new window with hundreds of name range options such as "Mike Hall–Mike Hirsch." You will need to keep using this drill-down method until you reach a list of actual profiles that meet your criteria. We do not enjoy this method, but sometimes it is all that we have. You may find your child this way after he used a misspelled version of his real name.

How do I search by location?

Twitter will allow you to search by a specific GPS location alone. The Twitter Advanced Search allowed you to search by zip code, but that can be too broad. The following specific search on any Twitter page will display tweets known to have been posted from within one kilometer of the GPS coordinates of 41.954169,-87.704677.

geocode: 41.954169,-87.704677,1km

There are no spaces in this search. This will be a list without any map view. They will be in order chronologically with the most recent at top. The "1km" indicates a search radius of one kilometer. This can be changed to 5, 10, or 25 reliably. Any other numbers tend to provide inaccurate results. You can also change "km" to "mi" to switch to miles instead of kilometers. You can add search parameters to either of these searches if the results are overwhelming. The following search would only display tweets posted at the listed GPS coordinates that also mention the term "fight." Notice that the only space in the above search is between "km" and "fight."

geocode: 41.954169,-87.704677,1km fight

This can be a very powerful tool for parents, but you will need to know the GPS coordinates of your desired search location. The easiest way to do this is with the help of Google Maps. While in Google Maps, search for the address of interest. This could be a home, school, or work address. When you do this, Google will place a small marker on top of the searched location on a map. Right-click on this location, and select "What's Here." The GPS coordinates of the searched location will appear near the bottom of the page.

You could use a Twitter location search in many ways. You may want to search your own address to see posts coming from within the house. You might want to monitor posts that originate at your child's school. Please remember that this technique only works if your child is sharing the location within the Twitter privacy settings on his or her phone. Many children purposely announce their locations, while some do so unknowingly. Many tech-savvy children disable this feature for more privacy.

One of the easiest location-based search websites for Twitter is a service called EchoSec at **app.echosec.net**. This premium Canadian website will display Twitter, Instagram, Panoramio, Foursquare, and Flickr data on one screen. While these additional networks will be explained later, this one-stop-shop is a great resource for this combined data. The free version mentioned here will only scour Twitter and Flickr. The main page will present a satellite view Google map focused on the San Francisco area. You can click the interactive map to navigate to a different area or type in an address in the search field. Once you have your area of interest visible on the map, click on the "Select Area" button and draw a box around the perimeter that you want to search. The map will populate with posts from the area and the markers will identify the social network. Below, you will see the content of your results. This will identify messages and photos from within the searched area. Figure 3.01 displays a search of a baseball stadium. Figure 3.02 displays the partial message results that appear below the map. The selection identifies the numerous posts from the inside of the stadium on the field.

Figure 3.01: Mapped results from a perimeter search on EchoSec.

20150922_174659
Cad Queen Karin
9/22/2015, 5:46:58 PM
via Flickr

20150922_174702
Cad Queen Karin
9/22/2015, 5:47:01 PM
via Flickr

20150922_174705
Cad Queen Karin
9/22/2015, 5:47:05 PM
via Flickr

Figure 3.02: Message results from a perimeter search on EchoSec.

Does my child share a location?

Whether you located your child's account by searching a location or completely struck out when searching your home address, you may still want to know if your child is announcing a location while tweeting. Most people post to Twitter through their smartphones. This allows users to take advantage of location aware apps such as Foursquare, which they can use to "check-in" to places and let their friends know their location. While privacy-aware individuals have disabled the location feature of their accounts, many children enjoy broadcasting their location at all times. Identifying your child's location during a Twitter post is sometimes possible through various methods. Please note that the following limited methods will only work if your target has not disabled the geolocate settings within Twitter.

The free online service GeoSocial Footprint, which is located at the website **www.geosocialfootprint.com**, will only search for location data within the most recent 200 posts. It is a good resource for identifying the current or recent location of your child, if available. Using this website is fairly straightforward and does not require a Twitter account. On the main page, enter your child's Twitter user name and click "Retrieve Tweets." This will produce a map with markers identifying the most recent locations of the child while posting. You can click on each marker to see the content of the message, but not the date and time. This overall view provides a quick glimpse into the general location of your child at a specific moment in time.

Can I search a specific date range?

If you are searching vague terms, you may want to filter by date. Assume that you are searching for a post that your child may have created several weeks or months ago. A search on Twitter of the terms "crazy party in Toronto" will likely apply only to recent posts. Instead, consider a date-specific search. The following query on any Twitter page would provide any posts that mention "crazy party in Toronto" between January 1, 2015 and January 5, 2015.

since:2015-01-01 until:2015-01-05 "crazy party in Toronto"

One favorite use of this search technique is to combine it with the "to" operator and a name search. This allows you to go further back in time than standard profile and Twitter feed searches typically allow. Consider an example where Twitter user ambermac is your child. You can visit her live Twitter page and navigate back through several thousand tweets. However, you will reach an end before obtaining all tweets. This could be due to Twitter restrictions or browser and computer limitations. Ambermac currently has 37.7 thousand tweets. Even if you could make it through all of her tweets, you are not seeing posts where she is mentioned or messages sent publicly to her. We recommend splitting this search by year and including mentions and messages directed toward her. The following search within Twitter displays all tweets from the Twitter name ambermac between January 1, 2012 and December 31, 2012.

from:ambermac since:2012-01-01 until:2012-12-31

This may create a more digestible collection of tweets. The following would display yearly sets of tweets posted by ambermac since 2006.

from:ambermac since:2006-01-01 until:2006-12-31
from:ambermac since:2007-01-01 until:2007-12-31
from:ambermac since:2008-01-01 until:2008-12-31
from:ambermac since:2009-01-01 until:2009-12-31
from:ambermac since:2010-01-01 until:2010-12-31
from:ambermac since:2011-01-01 until:2011-12-31
from:ambermac since:2012-01-01 until:2012-12-31
from:ambermac since:2013-01-01 until:2013-12-31
from:ambermac since:2014-01-01 until:2014-12-31
from:ambermac since:2015-01-01 until:2015-12-31

This same technique can be modified to display only incoming tweets to ambermac for these years. Replace "from" with "to" to obtain these results. The 2008 posts would appear as follows.

to:ambermac since:2008-01-01 until:2008-12-31

If your child posts to Twitter often, these search techniques may be vital in order to see everything. Using the "to" and "from" options allow you to focus only on incoming or outgoing messages. For parents new to Twitter, this isolation may help the digestion of hundreds of messages.

How long has my child been on Twitter?

In 2014, Twitter released a feature that allows you to view your child's first tweet at the website **discover.twitter.com/first-tweet**. This was designed to be fun and see how people started their Twitter accounts. You may be more interested in the date and time associated with this information. Each result includes the exact date and time of your child's first post. This helps identify the length of time he or she has been using a specific Twitter account.

What if my child deleted all of the tweets?

Did your child realize that you are monitoring Twitter and begin to delete posts? Twitter users may delete their own accounts or individual posts. If this happens, searching on Twitter will not display any of them. Furthermore, your child might only delete individual Twitter posts that are incriminating, but leave non-interesting posts on the profile to prevent raising suspicion associated with deleting an entire account. Some children may find their accounts suspended for violating Twitter's terms of service. In any of these scenarios, it is still possible to retrieve some missing posts using various techniques.

If you encounter a child's Twitter account that has recently deleted some or all of the messages, you can conduct a "cache" search of their profile. There are various ways to do this, and we will demonstrate the most common. As a controlled example, we conducted a search on Twitter for "just deleted all my tweets." This provided many users that recently posted that they had just deleted all of their content and helped us identify a good target for this type of demonstration. We reached out to Twitter user jeffgarlick and he agreed to participate.

Similar to the Facebook search methods described earlier, the following Twitter techniques may seem intrusive to some users. Retrieving content that a user believes has been deleted is completely legal, but it may upset the person who posted the content. You may want to consider limiting the following searches to only profiles associated with your immediate family members. Additionally, you should consider whether to disclose these techniques to your child or to protect them for future use. Once your child knows what you are capable of, the methods will become less effective.

On March 27, 2016, jeffgarlick deleted every tweet on his profile he could locate. He then posted a single tweet of "I just deleted all of my tweets. Time to start over again!" Figure 3.03 displays the view of his extremely limited account. Imagine that you have located your child's profile and encountered this disappointing result.

On March 28, 2016, with his permission, we searched many unconventional resources and were able to reconstruct much of the content that he assumed was gone forever. We first went to Google and conducted a search for "Twitter jeffgarlick." The first search result was a link to the user's live Twitter page. Instead of clicking on the link, we chose the Google Cache view of his profile by clicking the small green "down arrow" next to the profile address and selected "Cached." This option can be seen in Figure 3.04. This cached result identified dozens of deleted tweets from this account. This may be enough for your needs. Occasionally, you may want to identify messages that were deleted weeks or months before your discovery. The previous technique will likely not provide much assistance because the Google Cache is probably a recent copy of their live page. The cache will also be missing some tweets you want to see. For our next example, we navigated to Google and conducted the following exact search.

site:twitter.com/jeffgarlick

This instructed Google to search only the website twitter.com/jeffgarlick. Since Twitter creates an individual page for every tweet, and each of these pages start with twitter.com and then the person's user name, we should receive a large list of results. These results will include many individual messages that have been deleted from Twitter. Overall, Google located 52 unique Twitter post pages in reference to this target user name. These can be seen in Figure 3.04. When opening the links, we received a notification that the specific message had been removed from Twitter. Instead of clicking the live link, we clicked the "Cached" options for each, as explained previously.

We next visited the Twitter image search website Twicsy at **www.twicsy.com**. While searching within the designated search area might identify recent posts associated with the user name jeffgarlick, we went directly to his profile page. The following address displays any photos acquired by Twicsy from previous Twitter posts. You would replace jeffgarlick with your child's Twitter user name. The result is displayed in Figure 3.05.

www.twicsy.com/jeffgarlick

We decided to take a peek at three additional areas of Twitter data that many children do not realize is available after deleting all of their posts. The first involves incoming messages to the child. The main Twitter profile page displays outgoing posts by the user, but not necessarily incoming messages from others. If another child posted a tweet on his or her own profile, but directed it to your child (@), you may or may not see that post on your child's page. If your child removed everything, you definitely will not see any evidence of this content. However, it still exists. Using our volunteer, the following search on any Twitter page reveals these incoming messages sent to jeffgarlick. Figure 3.06 displays the result.

To:jeffgarlick

If your child has "Liked" any tweets, this data is searchable on Twitter. Whether his or her tweets are visible, this information may help you identify inappropriate behavior otherwise invisible from the profile view. Using our volunteer as an example, we visited the following exact website to see all of this content. As a reminder, he deleted everything within his account; however, these "Likes" will always be visible.

twitter.com/jeffgarlick/likes

Finally, we took a look at his media posts. These are tweets that include some form of media such as an image or video. Surprisingly, this recovered several messages that simply should not be obtainable. The following address displayed numerous posts.

twitter.com/jeffgarlick/media

Jeff kindly volunteered for this experiment, but imagine a scenario that involved your child. Recovering deleted tweets can be vital for investigative parents when they detect issues with their child. Ultimately, you should attempt these techniques sooner rather than later. As time passes, these methods become less reliable.

Is there an easier way of viewing this content?

You may find yourself using many of these manual Twitter search techniques daily. In order to prevent repetitive typing of the same addresses and searches, we present a custom web page with an all-in-one solution. Navigate to the website at **inteltechniques.com/osint/twitter.html** to access this resource. Figure 3.07 displays the current state of this tool. This tool will replicate many of the Twitter searches that you have read about here. The first option on the left side populates all of the search fields with your child's Twitter name when entered there. Clicking "Go" next to each option executes the query in a new tab in your browser. We recommend executing all search options using your child's Twitter name.

Figure 3.03: A tweet indicating deletion.

Figure 3.04: A Google result page with cached view option.

Figure 3.05: A Twicsy archive of deleted images.

Figure 3.06: Tweets sent to a user that deleted all posts.

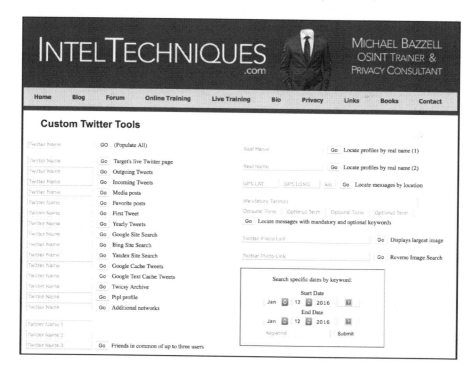

Figure 3.07: The IntelTechniques Custom Twitter Search Tool.

How can I easily view and save all of my child's posts?

The website All My Tweets at **www.allmytweets.net** provides a clean display of all of your child's Twitter posts on one screen. It will start with the most recent post and list previous posts on one line each. This view will display up to 3200 messages on one scrollable screen. This provides an easier option for digesting large amounts of posts. Holding CTRL and F on the keyboard will present a search box. Any search terms can be entered to navigate directly to associated messages. You may want to search specific problem topics such as "fight," "weed," or "parents." This also eliminates the need to constantly load more tweets at the end of every page throughout a profile.

All My Tweets can be a great resource for locating posts published by your target. However, it will only show you one side of the conversation. You would need to perform the same action on every user associated with your child. The website Conweets at **www.conweets.com** may eliminate this problem. This website allows you to enter two Twitter users and it will identify the conversations between them. It will display their tweets in order from most recent to the oldest. Each section will identify the person that started the conversation and the date. The appearance is similar to a back-and-forth text message session. It can give parents a better understanding of the context associated with tweets from a conversation. Figure 3.08 displays a result.

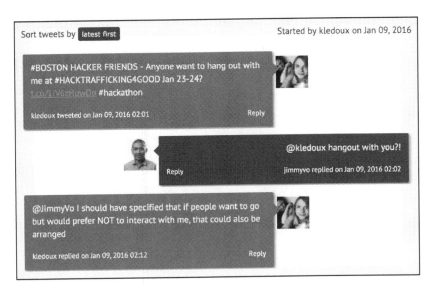

Figure 3.08: A conversation on Conweets.

When does my child usually tweet?

The website Sleeping Time at **www.sleepingtime.org** allows for a search of your child's Twitter profile name, and provides the average time period that he or she commonly sleeps. The historical tweets are analyzed according to the times of posts. Data is then presented that suggests when he or she is usually sleeping due to lack of posting during a specific time period. A query of Kevin Mitnick revealed that he is likely to be sleeping between 12am and 7am according to his tweets. Although the idea was probably executed as a fun site, it can be quite useful in determining your child's sleep patterns.

Can I watch my child tweet in real-time?

The website TweetDeck located at **www.tweetdeck.com** is owned by Twitter, and it can take advantage of the Twitter "Firehose" in real-time. This huge stream of data contains every public post available on Twitter. TweetDeck requires you to log into an account to use the service. The "Create Account" button on the website will walk you through the process. After logging in, the plus symbol (+) in the upper left area will add a new column to your view. There are several options presented, but the most common will be "Search" and "User." The "Search" option will create a column that will allow you to search for any keywords on Twitter. The result will automatically refresh on your screen as new content is posted online. The following is a list of search examples and how they may benefit parents. The category inside quotation marks should be replaced with terms relevant to your situation.

"School Name": You can monitor anyone mentioning your child's school for suspicious activity. This will likely come from students who attend the school, possibly your own children.

"Child's Name": You can monitor your own child's name for relevant information being posted by other children. This will often identify bullying issues.

"Child's Twitter Name": You can monitor your own child's Twitter user name for any mentions of it within Twitter. This can identify outgoing tweets by the child or incoming tweets from other children.

"Event": You can monitor anyone discussing a special event such as a school festival or concert. This can reveal potential problems brewing at the event such as violence or vandalism.

The "User" search option will allow you to enter a Twitter user name and monitor all outgoing public messages associated with the user. This may sound redundant considering the previous method that explained a similar approach. However, this method will provide a single column that displays posts from your child's account. The previous method looks for posts that contain your child's user name. In a moment, we will share our ideal setup.

If several children associated with your child are identified as Twitter users, each of the profiles can be loaded in a separate column and monitored. Occasionally, this will result in two of the profiles communicating with each other while being monitored. If your child is tweeting another child who you are monitoring, you will see both sides of the conversation. This method is vital if you identify online bullying targeted toward, or coming from, your child.

You can also use the Geo search mentioned earlier within TweetDeck. A column that searches "geocode:43.430242,-89.736459,1km" will display a live feed of tweets posted within the specified range. A more precise search of "geocode:43.430242,-89.736459,1km fight" would add the keyword to filter the results that only included the word "fight." Figure 3.09 displays one instance of TweetDeck with a combination of search types.

The Ideal TweetDeck Setup

You may be overwhelmed at the numerous options with TweetDeck. We are here to help. Assume that your child's Twitter user name is AmberMac, she attends Unionville High School, and is being bullied by a Twitter user named MBancroft80. We recommend a total of eight columns within TweetDeck configured as follows, without the quotation marks. The terms "Search" and "User" identify which TweetDeck option to choose when creating a new column.

Search: "AmberMac": This column will display any tweet that contains AmberMac within the content of the message. It may identify people mentioning your child without actually targeting the post toward her.

Search: "To:AmberMac": This will display every public tweet that is directed toward your child from another user. This will include messages meant for her to read.

Search: "Unionville": This will display every tweet that mentions the school. While this may be an overwhelming feed, it can identify daily problems that could impact your child.

User: "AmberMac": This will display your child's live account stream.

User: "MBancroft80": This will display the bully's live account stream.

Search "to:MBancroft80": This will display incoming messages to the bully that may be relevant to your situation.

Search: "geocode: 43.858359, -79.336641,1km": Placing the GPS coordinates of the school will display any geotagged tweets from within one kilometer of the school. While some will be from surrounding areas that are not associated with the desired location, many will be from students on site.

Search: "geocode: 43.858359, -79.336641,1km": Placing the GPS coordinates of your home might display tweets coming from your child's phone or the devices of her visitors.

The columns of TweetDeck are consistently sized. If more columns are created than can fit in the display, the "Columns" option with left and right arrows will provide navigation. This allows for numerous search columns regardless of screen resolution. TweetDeck is one of our Twitter staples. We use it at some point weekly. We recommend familiarizing yourself with all of the features before needing to rely on it during your searches of your child's online interactions.

Figure 3.09: A TweetDeck search screen.

Summary

With tips and tools from the above section, you should now be able to find your child on Twitter, monitor their usage, and retrieve deleted tweets. This will help you to keep an eye on how they are interacting on Twitter, discover what location information they are sharing, and determine their circle of friends on this particular platform. As we mentioned at the beginning of this chapter, Twitter is evolving beyond 140 characters and is now home to user images and videos. Plus, as we'll discuss in Chapter Five, the company's six-second video app Vine is experiencing phenomenal growth. As of the summer of 2015, Vine reported 200 million monthly active users.

While there are plenty of dangers associated with sharing on Twitter, there are also a number of benefits. In fact, depending on your child's age, there are plenty of interesting people and educational content for them to follow. In other words, while you should be sweeping social media services to monitor your kids, it's also a good idea to embrace the positive elements of these platforms (which do exist!).

With Twitter, for example, you might want to spend some time with your child to recommend a few of the following accounts.

Top 10 Twitter Accounts for Families

@NASA: With more than 15 million followers, this account includes multiple daily updates about what's happening in space. They regularly post gorgeous photos that include everything from a disorganized dwarf galaxy to Pluto's strangest features. However, probably one of the most exciting features of this account is their regular astronaut updates; Scott Kelly made frequent appearances here, but you can also follow him (along with his one million fans!) @StationCDRKelly.

@BillNye: More than two million people follow one the world's most famous scientists. If your kids want to learn from someone who has decades of experience and a witty way of looking at the world, @BillNye is the guy. With his famous bow tie, he also enchants his followers with short video clips and the latest climate change news. Perhaps the wisest words are in his Twitter bio, "Everyone you will ever meet knows something you don't."

@ArtForKidsHub: Dad Rob and his three kids share their latest step-by-step artwork on this account with detailed tutorials so children can easily recreate each featured project. This account is especially relevant for preschoolers and young preteens who like to model other creative kids. Whether you want to learn how to draw Chewbacca or paint a parrot, it's all here on Twitter.

@GoogleArt: On the topic of art, Google has a place on Twitter with this interactive account. Regular updates here include exhibits and collections from the most visited museums around the world. Aside from a steady stream of beautiful images, they also share historical art in GIF format.

@History_Pics: While reading through this Twitter feed might seem like fun, it's also a good visual history lesson. This popular account includes "good and bad, fun and sad moments from bygone times." From an image from the streets of Philadelphia celebrating the end of WWII, to a long-haired George Harrison circa 1970, this is the place to send your teens for a fun trip down memory lane.

@ajplus: If your older teens are showing some interest in the news, there is no better place for them to stay on top of what's happening in the world than AJ+. This account shares the planet's most timely stories with young hosts, short videos, and colorful slideshows. In short, if your child doesn't want to read a newspaper, but needs to stay on top of politics and more, this is the place where they can do it in just a few minutes a day.

@HowStuffWorks: "If I plant trees in my yard, will it offset global warming?" This account will answer questions just like this to teach your kids how stuff works. From sleep myths to fishing dangers, this feed dishes out facts and stats on today's most interesting topics. Plus, if you've ever needed to know why a wombat scat is shaped like a cube, they will tell you in 140 characters.

@HannahAlper: If your preteen is looking for inspiration from today's pop icons, you might want to redirect them to some of today's youngest motivational tweeters. Thirteen-year-old Hannah Alper has a dedicated following of kids who are interested in how to make the world a more positive place. She addresses many current issues such as what to do about bullying, but all from a young person's point of view.

@Pottermore: For Harry Potter fans, this account is a dream come true.

More than 1.5 million people follow @Pottermore for the digital tidbits from J.K. Rowling's famous series. This includes everything from reader polls to exclusive artwork. One of the best things about this account is that it's not just a one-way conversation, the creators respond regularly to their legion of fans.

@SesameStreet: Parents can share some of their findings from this account with their youngest at home. For *Sesame Street* fans, this is the place to go to learn about the organization's latest initiatives. Plus, you will get a first look at their modern new stars and latest digital offerings. Moms and dads will also get some good lessons from Sesame Street's talented roster of parenting experts.

In the next chapter we will dive into one of the fastest growing social media communities for preteens and teens, Instagram.

A Question from a Parent

Darryl Ricker: How do I give my teenager some level of privacy, while still having some control over what they're doing online, or is that even possible or wise?

Amber's Answer: It is possible to give your child some privacy while also monitoring what they're doing online. This is one of the reasons that we've recommended a service later in the book called VISR, which simply scans and flags issues that they see across your child's social media account. Also, although you may be monitoring what your child is doing online, that doesn't mean that you have to nag them about every single thing that you see. If you want to respect their privacy, simply worry about the things that could put them in a dangerous situation. If, after following some of our monitoring strategies throughout the book, you find that your kid is using the Internet responsibly, you can back off with your deep-dive and simply check in on a regular basis. For generations, parents have always employed different tactics to keep their kids safe; whether it's calling a mom to confirm a sleepover or watching what your child is doing on Instagram, it's all part of the job.

Chapter Four
Instagram Concerns

The first photo on Instagram was not a filtered selfie, as one might expect, but instead a random dog chilling at a taco stand. The company's CEO and co-founder Kevin Systrom took the picture and shared it on July 16, 2010, long before #dogsofinstagram became a trending hashtag. By December of that same year, Instagram grew steadily to attract more than one million users. At that time, not many users thought of the popular new service with a funny name as a social network at all. For most, it was a hip new photography app that made it easy for people to add filters that were at one time reserved for only true Photoshop professionals.

Initially, the app launched for iOS users only, but eventually it became available for other platforms. In the spring of 2012, Facebook announced they were acquiring Instagram for approximately $1 billion. This news made headlines all over the world and was a major milestone for the Facebook platform as it would mark the beginning of the company's aggressive move to buy what they could not quickly make. As another example, Facebook recently bought the face-swapping app MSQRD (Masquerade) to take on Snapchat's filters.

Of course, it wasn't just the technology they were buying, it never is; it was Instagram's millions of users. While photo sharing was an important feature on Facebook, nothing could compare to how Instagram users were flocking to this new platform and rapidly turning it into a top social media destination.

The mere idea that an app-based community could compete with Facebook's web platform was a sign of things to come on the mobile front. The rise of Instagram signified a major move for users into smartphone-first experiences, no doubt inspired by younger technology users who didn't want to be tethered to desktop computers. Preteens and teens were also demonstrating that they were hungry for more and more visual content. Every new device launched in 2010 had some sort of camera capability, so Instagram finally allowed them to share their lives in slick square snapshots (with pretty filters to hide life's imperfections).

Today, Facebook's acquisition is proving to be one of the smartest moves the company has made. As of September 2015, Instagram boasts 400 million users. The company has expanded well beyond images. In the summer of 2013, they added the option to upload fifteen-second video clips so the community there can now look–and watch. They've also recently expanded that video limit to one minute, indicating that the company sees advertising in photo and video format as an ongoing revenue opportunity.

Kids Heart Instagram

For parents, it's Instagram's adoption among new, younger audiences that is particularly telling and relevant. In 2015, Pew Research Center discovered that 52 percent of teens between the ages of 13 to 17 use Instagram on a regular basis (other recent surveys show this number to be even higher, sometimes closing in on 70 percent). For this age group, this particular social network is the second most popular in terms of usage (just behind Facebook). Again, with Facebook's Instagram acquisition, that means that the two services are closely integrated and there is constant cross-posting from Instagram to Facebook.

Preteens are also flocking to Instagram. In some cases, this age group is bypassing Facebook entirely and using this service as their number one mobile destination. Although the service has a 13-year-old sign-up minimum, which is similar to other social networks, plenty of younger children are using Instagram in creative ways. Amber knows a 10-year-old girl who uses the app to document her family travels, posting special moments such as swimming in the Atlantic Ocean for the first time and eating lobster with her grandparents. She relies on Instagram as a daily diary, filled with beautiful photos of her daily adventures. As we explain below, these habits will undoubtedly change, so parents need to understand the intricate layers of Instagram in order to provide guidance to these young users at home.

Girls and Visual Social Media

As we mentioned earlier in the book, girls tend to be more active on visual social media. This is especially true on sites such as Instagram that focus on images and video. As girls get older, their relationship with Instagram (and the Internet) gets more complicated. The images and videos are no longer the sole focus of the experience, but instead the comments attached to them start to tell a different story about how these teens are building, and in some cases destroying relationships. Furthermore, this age group starts to demonstrate strong attention-seeking behavior (the need for likes and compliments). This is often also the beginning of sharing sexy and inappropriate photos, which can elicit unwanted attention from people these girls know—and even more worrisome—from people they don't know.

A report from UK-based Schools Health Education Unit recently blamed social media for a "crisis of confidence" among British school girls. They found that in the past seven years, just 33 percent of 14- and 15-year-old girls felt good about themselves (compared to 41 percent just seven years prior). Girls in this age group struggle with the way they look, reporting that they often eat very little in order to lose weight (#skinny is a popular Instagram theme yielding easily five million results a day). Researchers say this is most definitely connected to today's emphasis on visual social media. Even more disturbing, this same study found that one in five 14- and 15-year-old girls chatted with someone online they didn't know.

The Girl Scout Research Institute has also studied the connection between girls and social media, indicating that 68 percent of girls have had a negative experience online (including bullying and harassment). If you do a quick Google search about Instagram dangers, you will quickly discover headlines such as this March 2016 story from the *Las Vegas Sun*, "Man used Instagram to lure, sexually assault girl, 13."

The 21-year-old man allegedly blackmailed the young girl and threatened to tell her mom about their Instagram conversations if she didn't agree to meet him. Fortunately, after some time, the young girl's mother was able to intervene after another mother got hold of some social media messages and told her what was happening. This could have ended tragically if this second mother didn't intervene.

Later in the book we discuss how this man's approach is far too common and what to do if you discover something like this happening to a young member of your family.

Challenges and Opportunities

If we think back to teenage life before Instagram, there were plenty of examples of bullying and harassment, and a long list of incidents that involved predators and attacks. The biggest difference in today's digital world is the always-on nature of technology and these social media services.

As one of Amber's friends explains, when he was a young teen boy he was frequently bullied at school for being gay. However, he knew that when he came home after school (remember, this is pre-Internet) he had an escape from those people. He could leave school and leave the bullies behind. Preteens, and especially teens, are now connected to technology around the clock. If you have a child at home in this age group, you're probably struggling to get them to disconnect at bedtime. There are daily stories about teens who are so hooked on the Internet that they put their phones in Ziplock bags so they can use them in the shower. Yes, these are challenging times.

We mentioned in the Twitter chapter that, beyond the dangers, there are also some compelling reasons to use social media. If we look at Instagram, there are plenty of inspiring and educational accounts to follow. Take a look at Amy Poehler's *Smart Girls* (@AmyPoehlerSmartGirls), a community created by Amy Poehler and her best friend Meredith Walker. Their goal is to help girls be their truest selves, and they work hard on social media to share images and content to reinforce this with their fans. If you take a look back at our Twitter list of ten accounts for kids (and parents!) to follow, you will find that many of these users are also on Instagram; @NASA, @BillNye, and @ArtForKidsHub are just three examples of accounts to follow on this image-based platform for some excellent content.

In this chapter, we will provide you with the tools and techniques you need to monitor what your kids are doing on Instagram. This includes how to find their Instagram account; how to do a search by keyword; what to do if their account is private; and how to dig up examples of location information they're sharing. Before we dive into the information, we want to talk about commonly used terms on Instagram and what they mean to your kids.

Please keep in mind that most of these terms refer to everyday Instagram lingo, but kids also work hard to develop their own secret language and hashtags on the service. For example, back in 2012, there was a rise in the number of posts among young people who were promoting and glorifying self-harm. As a result, Instagram created new guidelines against self-harm images and accounts. The company explains online:

"While Instagram is a place where people can share their lives with others through photographs, any account found encouraging or urging users to embrace anorexia, bulimia, or other eating disorders; or to cut, harm themselves, or commit suicide will result in a disabled account without warning. We believe that communication regarding these behaviors in order to create awareness, come together for support and to facilitate recovery is important, but that Instagram is not the place for active promotion or glorification of self-harm."

Although this ban can in no way fix the problem entirely, if you search #selfharm on Instagram there are 0 results thanks to this policy. However, searching "site:instagram.com #selfharm" on Google identifies over 7,000 posts on Instagram with this keyword. While Instagram blocks this type of search, Google does not. Tech-savvy children know these search workarounds. Additionally, kids are always creative and will start to develop their own hashtags, adding letters and numbers to banned search terms or dreaming up new ways to describe something against the company's guidelines. In short, don't assume that an innocent-sounding hashtag is all that innocent. A good search, which we will show you how to do later in this chapter, will uncover images revealing the tag's true meaning.

Instagram Terminology Parents Need to Know

At this point, most people are familiar with the terms user name (or handle), hashtag, follow, like, and the @ symbol. Here is a quick list of some more frequently used words and symbols you will discover on Instagram.

IG: This is short form for Instagram. Although it's a pretty obvious one, it's worth mentioning as there is an increase in how much it is used on users' bios on other social media sites to reference their activity on Instagram. It can also be used as slang, such as "I'll add you on IG," or "FMOIG" which refers to "Follow me on IG."

Filter: This is Instagram's most famous feature. When uploading a photo, you then touch the arrow in the upper right side of the screen to add any of the app's popular filters. These include Valencia, Lo-Fi, and many more filters that will give your image a unique look. The company regularly releases new filters to keep its users engaged.

Caption: When you post an image on Instagram, you can add descriptive text below the photo; this text is called a caption. This is the most common way that users give images context. It's also the place where users include hashtags so their images are searchable by a wider audience. Just another quick note on hashtags; although these started as one-word tags, they are frequently expanded into full phrases or sayings. There is more on hashtags below.

Photo Map: When you choose a location to add to your photo, this automatically includes your image in Instagram's photo map. We will talk about this further below, but keep in mind that if your Instagram account is not private and you do allow geotagging on your photos, anyone can see where these photos have been taken. These photos will also appear on a location page that anyone can browse. Instagram gives some location sharing advice in their help section, but it reads more like a warning: "We ask that you're mindful of which photos you add to your photo map since the precise locations of your photos and videos are visible to anyone who can see your posts." Nonetheless, many users continue to post location information—even when it includes their home street.

Activity Feed: This is the place where you will be able to see all the action on your feed. For example, if a user likes your photo or comments on your photo, you can see that information here. This is similar to the News Feed on Facebook.

Instagram Direct: When Instagram initially launched, there was no way to privately message a user. They have since created something called Instagram Direct, which gives you direct messaging functionality. Within Instagram Direct, you can also privately share photos or videos from your camera roll. This is often where problems start in terms of exchanges of inappropriate content from friends or strangers. It's also easy to privately share a post that someone has posted publicly. While some users may not realize this, it is possible to unsend a message you've sent so it is no longer viewable (unless, of course, that person has taken a screenshot). To unsend a message, you tap and hold a message and press Unsend. Finally, you can also send direct messages to groups of people.

Repost: There are a number of third-party apps that allow you to repost an image, which means you can share someone's post and caption within your own feed. There are a couple of scenarios when you might want to do this.

If you are following a fashion brand, for example, you may want to share a photo of a new swimsuit from the company's Instagram account with your friends on Instagram.

Hashtags: Hashtags on Instagram perform the same way as they do on other social media sites, such as Twitter. In fact, Instagram's explosive popularity is dependent in part on how its users rely on hashtags to share and search. There are a number of well-used hashtags that are worth inspection so that you're familiar with them when you're reviewing your child's account. For more, check out this website: **http://top-hashtags.com/instagram.**

Instagram Hashtags Parents Need to Know

#TBT: Throw Back Thursday is a tag often used when, on a Thursday, a user shares a photo that took place in the past. Initially, this trend started when users were posting old-school pictures, such as their graduation photos or a childhood birthday party.

#OOTD: A term such as this can look kind of confusing at first, but this one is pretty innocent. It means Outfit of the Day. Instagram is a hot destination for fashion lovers (#fashion is often the most popular tag), so this hashtag lets a user post a photo of his or her daily outfit.

#FoodPorn: This one is fairly obvious, although it is always disturbing to see the word porn on a young child's Instagram account. In this case, there is no need to be overly concerned. This hashtag simply refers to photos of delicious looking food, such as "Check out my Oreo flavored Dairy Queen Blizzard #FoodPorn."

#PRON: This tag has two letters reversed to prevent it from being censored. The misspelled word here represents "porn" and is often tagged to offensive sexual content. The list of creative hashtags describing banned material is endless and not always as obvious as this one example.

#GNRN: This abbreviation stands for "get naked right now" and is frequently grouped with the tag GNOC (get naked on camera). Alarm bells should be going off if you see this in your child's account. They could be experiencing unwanted pressure from peers or posting inappropriate content to encourage such remarks.

#TINA: Innocent looking enough and could refer to a friend in the photo. Or it could be a reference to the drug crystal meth. Consider the context of the photo before jumping to conclusions.

#Regram: This is similar to reposting an image. It simply means that the original image was found in another user's feed, so this is a way to acknowledge the source.

#Fitspo: As we mentioned above, Instagram is home to a number of people who are working hard to inspire healthy living. This tag is often used below photos of men and women who are working out and eating in a sensible way. If you see the tag #thinspo, this often refers to (and is posted by) someone with an eating disorder. Instagram has a lengthy Help section on its website detailing what signs to look for if a friend may have an eating disorder–tips you can use to intervene and help, and resources that will give you more information. While all of this guidance is available for free, it's unlikely your child will locate this helpful content, so it's a good idea to send them this way if this topic comes up or if you're concerned.

#NoFilter: Although Instagram is famous for its filters, there are many users who prefer to use the tag #NoFilter to showcase an image's natural, untouched beauty.

#ImCrying: While this might seem like a worrisome tag, it usually means that a user is laughing so hard they are crying. In other words, this doesn't necessarily mean your son or daughter is upset.

There are plenty more hashtags that are commonly used on Instagram. A quick Google search will lead you to definitions for most of these popular terms and tags.

How do I find my child's Instagram account?

There is no user name search feature on the Instagram home page. If you want to use Instagram's user search database, you must connect directly to an account such as Instagram.com/ambermac and use the search field at the top of the page. This search field identifies profiles related to the search terms provided. You can type in a suspected user name of your child and view any related results.

Our preferred Instagram user name search resource is IconoSquare at the website **www.iconosquare.com**. If you know only a partial user name of your child, it can be searched on any page within the site. The result is a list of every Instagram account that contains the exact characters entered. This is helpful if your child also has profiles named ambermac4, ambermac9, etc.

How do I search Instagram by keyword?

There is no content search feature on the Instagram home page or individual profiles. The search field explained previously only identifies users related to the search terms. It does not provide a true keyword search. For this, you must rely on traditional search engines and third party services. We have found the best success with a custom Google search instead of an Instagram search field. The following query on Google will produce numerous results that display Instagram posts that mention "Michael Bazzell." These same terms searched in Instagram directly produced 0 user results. Figure 4.01 displays an example of a Google search that identified 10,300 Instagram posts that contain the terms "kill myself."

site:instagram.com "Michael Bazzell"

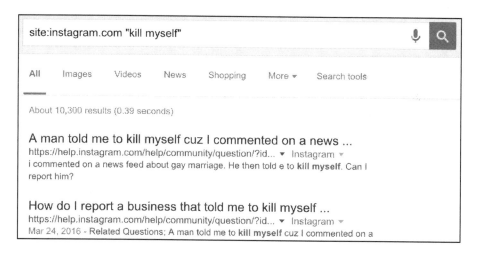

Figure 4.01: A Google search for Instagram posts.

Michael's Hacks

What if my child's account is "Private"?

There is no official way of displaying Instagram posts of a child who has made his or her profile private. However, two techniques might be beneficial if a child posts through other social networks. As an example, assume your child has a private Instagram account at instagram.com/johnnyb. This private account only reveals a profile photo in the upper left area and general details about him. The posts are all blocked from any user who johnnyb has not given permission to to follow him. The following two methods should be attempted individually.

The profile photo is a 150x150 pixel image that is small and heavily compressed. In 2015, Instagram changed the way that these thumbnails and original images are stored. The goal of this technique is to locate these small thumbnail images; identify the full high resolution images that were originally uploaded; and locate additional copies of the image online. In our example, when you right click on the profile picture, and choose "open image in new tab" (Chrome Browser) or "view the image" (Firefox Browser), you are presented with a new tab within your web browser that contains only that image. The address of the image may appear similar to the following.

https://scontent.cdninstagram.com/hphotos-xtp1/t51/s150x150/910_a.jpg

Note the portion that displays s150x150. This is telling Instagram to retrieve the 150-pixel thumbnail for your child and display it. If you remove that portion of the URL, you will receive a much different result. Instead, you would load the following URL (address).

https://scontent.cdninstagram.com/hphotos-xtp1/t51/910_a.jpg

The result is the original profile image uploaded by your child at full resolution. The detail of this image trumps the original thumbnail presented with the profile. You will want to conduct a "reverse image search" of this image with hopes of finding other accounts that also use this image, likely from your child.

One of the more powerful reverse image search services is through Google. Rolled out in 2011, this service often goes undetected. On any Google Images page at **images.google.com**, there is a search field. Inside this field on the far right is a light grey camera icon that appears slightly transparent. Clicking on this icon will open a new search window that will allow for entering either an address of an online image, or an upload of an image file from your computer.

In order to take advantage of the online search, you must have the exact link to the actual Instagram profile photo, as described previously. If you paste this link in the Google Images reverse online search, the result will be other similar images of your child, or exact duplicate images, on other sites. Visiting these sites provides more information on him or her.

If you are unsuccessful in locating public content from your child with a reverse image search, a second method has a higher success rate. If you know your child's Twitter account user name, head to that webpage. If you don't know the Twitter name, conduct a search on Google of your child's Instagram user name followed by the term "Twitter." This will likely present an immediate result that links to your child's Twitter page. Open the Twitter profile and press CTRL-F (Windows) or COMMAND-F (Mac). This will present a search field at the top of your browser. Type the word "Instagram" and scroll through any results. These will likely be links to posts on the private Instagram profile. Why does this work? Instagram profiles can be set to private and will block you from seeing any content. However, the individual posts are actually public. Since many children share their Instagram posts to the world via Twitter, you can often intercept this content believed to be protected.

Is my child announcing a location within Instagram posts?

The free website Yomapic located at **www.yomapic.com** appears very similar to the service Echosec that was discussed in Chapter Three. However, this option presents Instagram posts that possess GPS information within an online map. The simple interface allows for a text search by location name or an interactive map that can be used to select a specific point. After choosing a location of interest, the right column will populate with photos posted from the area. Pink markers on the satellite view identify the locations of each post. The results usually include the most recent posts at the top and posts from previous weeks toward the bottom. Similar to earlier methods for locating tweets that contain location data, we recommend that you search by familiar locations including your child's home, school, and workplace.

Summary

Now you have the strategies you need to search Instagram to find your child's account, and make sense of what they're sharing with their friends online (whether they're using official Instagram terms or Internet slang). One thing to note, there is a Parents' Guide to Instagram on the company's website. This Guide is customized for several different countries around the world, including the United States, Canada, and Australia. Most of the tips offered are fairly basic and are presented with a pro-Instagram filter, no pun intended. In other words, they very strongly encourage photo sharing and don't dive too deeply into some of the more serious problems that can occur on this platform. However, as we mentioned above, within the larger Instagram Privacy & Safety Center, you can learn how to address abuse, share photos safely, and report something that is against the company's policy. In the Parents' Guide, there is a section worth highlighting called "How you represent yourself." This includes five main points, but it's the latter three that we want to expand on here.

Consider the whole image

This is an especially important point to discuss with your teen. While the speed and efficiencies of smartphone cameras are impressive, sometimes we're too quick to snap and share. This means, as Instagram mentions, that you should consider what's in the background of the photo or the video you're taking (not just your main subjects).

Whether your son is capturing a shot on your front doorstep and inadvertently includes your home's street number, or your daughter is taking a selfie at a friend's party and fails to notice someone rolling a joint on a table behind her, it's important to consider the entirety of the image. While we haven't talked extensively about this yet, we need to reinforce that parents must also set a good example on Instagram for their children. In Chapter 10: Parent Patrol, we talk further about online etiquette for all members of the family.

Your media could show up anywhere

Although Instagram dedicates just two sentences to this point, it's worth stressing to young Instagram users at home that Instagram is primarily a public sharing platform. That means the company purposefully makes it easy to embed an Instagram photo or video on any website online. This is advantageous to Instagram as it helps to build their brand, but it could be hurtful to your child if he or she expected that the content would remain exclusively within the Instagram platform.

Whether your child limits the Instagram audience for their media or not, we all know how easy it is for someone to quickly snap a screenshot and distribute this material online. Also, according to a recent Jobvite survey, keep in mind that 92 percent of recruiters use social media to research information about a potential candidate. Thirteen percent actively search Instagram, and this number is already starting to rise. Although it might be difficult to convince your child that social media can hurt them down the road when they're looking for a job, remind them that college and university recruiters also deploy the same tactics.

Use a strong password, and don't share it

Many of Instagram's youngest users share passwords. They don't do this because they want someone to have a back-up in case they can't access their account, but instead they do this for unique personal reasons. Yes, they swap passwords as a sign of trust. It's not difficult to imagine how quickly this can backfire, whether a friend takes over your daughter's account and posts embarrassing photos or a friend takes over your son's account and regrams sexually explicit content.

Pew Research Center found that 19 percent of teens share their social media passwords with friends. As the think tank explains in their report on this topic, "A high school girl in one of our focus groups described a social media game that highlights this: 'I know they have this game on Instagram where you'd be like, 'do you trust me? Give me your password and I'll post a picture and then log back off.'" As we've mentioned a number of times above, a young person's relationship with the Internet is complicated; when they give someone else their password, it also gets dangerous.

While it might seem like investing time in learning about Instagram to the level we've described above is unnecessary since children bounce from one social network to another, within this book we are focusing dedicated chapters on the social networking services that we know have longevity. Instagram is also proving that it can adapt quickly to meet young user demand. As co-founder Systrom described to *TIME.com* on the company's fifth birthday, the power of Instagram is also that it appeals to a diverse group of users who span generations and interests.

"The next decade, at least on Instagram, will be the decade where we realize the power of a collective group of people capturing the world in real-time through their phones," he explains. "I don't think we quite understand how that will disrupt industries, whether that's news [or] how we consume events happening around the world. And I hope that Instagram can become a platform and a medium that accelerates that disruption, and accelerates that access to everything happening in the world in real-time. It's going to be fun to see."

He also points out in this article that video is a crucial part of our social media future—and Instagram's success. To address some of the challenges parents face when their kids start watching and creating online videos, check out our next chapter. This includes strategies you need to manage your child on YouTube, Vine, Periscope, and other video-based services.

A Question from a Parent

Meegan Thomas: I wish there was a way to stop kids from creating multiple accounts online. Since we teach kids not to use their own name or favorite passwords for setting up accounts, it's easy for them to have multiple accounts without anyone knowing. What can parents do?

Amber's Answer: That is a great point. Smart kids hide their true identity online as a safety precaution. This can be challenging for parents. We recommend looking at your child's browsing history in order to locate unknown social network profiles. Visiting the websites in this history view will likely display any profiles that were created or updated from that computer. While each web browser is different, going to the "Tools" menu should point you in the right direction.

Chapter Five
Online Video

If you think monitoring what your kids are messaging on Facebook or Twitter is hard, prepare yourself for the chaotic world of online video. Unlike parents, today's kids don't necessarily distinguish between TV, film, and Internet content. If you remember in our main introduction, we refer to this youngest generation of web users as the Screeners; they have been, in one way or another, exposed to screens since birth. They choose their media on demand and it travels with them wherever they go. To this generation, appointment television is the equivalent of a party line. If you're too young to remember the latter, it's a telephone line shared by two or more subscribers.

Parental advice for other types of entertainment is much more sophisticated than parental advice for online video (of which there is virtually none). Take *Common Sense Media*, for example, it is a wonderful resource to discover age-appropriate movies, games, apps, websites, TV shows, books, and music. Have an 8-year-old at home? The site makes it a cinch to sift through more than 100 popular websites and quickly discover their educational rating. However, if you search for DanTDM on this same site, you will get zero results.

DanTDM is a wildly popular YouTuber who started making videos in 2012 and now has more than 10 million subscribers. He creates tutorials for popular games such as Minecraft, which lets kids design and build using animated cubes. As Amber's 7-year-old son Connor says, "DanTDM used to have some inappropriate content, but now he knows kids are watching so he warns you if there are violent parts." In other words, the kids are policing the kids because the adults are rarely in the equation.

While we're focusing on online video, it's important to remember that for most children the distribution platforms are meaningless. For example, let's take a look at the above Minecraft scenario. Amber's son doesn't just watch DanTDM on YouTube. He watches this popular channel on an iPad with his notebook on his lap. As Connor is watching, he is also building what he is learning from DanTDM in his own Minecraft world. He can connect on a local network so friends visiting his house can play along. If Connor wants to take his world with him to a friend's house, he can load it onto a USB bracelet called Gameband and transport it neatly and safely on his wrist. At his friend's house, Connor and his buddies can then use the laptop's web camera to create their own videos showcasing their Minecraft creation to DanTDM through the comments section to earn his respect, attention, and approval.

Consuming, Creating, and Community

Consuming online video is rarely a passive activity for kids. You won't see them making a bowl of popcorn, turning out the lights, switching off their phones, and hunkering down to catch their favorite show at 9pm on a Thursday night. This means children are most often consuming AND creating—seamlessly switching back and forth. While this multi-tasking used to be limited to services such as YouTube, today's preschoolers, preteens, and teens are the key drivers behind the rise of fragmented content viewing and creating.

The final part of this equation is community. On YouTube, and other video platforms, there is most often a flock of fans attached to each platform. You will meet them in the comments section. When you read the feedback on pretty much any popular video online, you are easily pulled into a sea of toxicity. Take our popular YouTuber DanTDM. He has more than 10 million subscribers, a stat the traditional TV networks covet, but is still the victim of online vitriol.

A quick scan through his comments and you will find one user calling him an "idiot" and another saying "10 mill subs so underserved." On the flip side, there is also an army of fans who regularly come to his defense. One such fan lashes out at a hater saying, "imma send a kitten assassination team after you." When the number of comments reaches in the tens of thousands on each video, as it does with DanTDM, there are plenty of them that are actually quite threatening.

Online Video Apps

Later in this chapter, we will discuss micro video services such as Vine, which is owned by Twitter, and what parents need to know. We will talk to Internet celeb Stewart Reynolds, AKA @Brittlestar, about his advice for families who want to safely create Vines together. On the live streaming front, services such as Periscope, which Twitter also owns, are growing rapidly. We will dive further into how this app works. To put its popularity in context, here are some numbers. In its first year online, Periscope hosted more than 200 million broadcasts. They continue to be one of the leading apps in what is a very young industry.

Vine is a popular app that lets you create brief six-second videos. When the service initially went online, many users simply downloaded the app to upload random clips (think short videos of dogs doing tricks).

For example, the very first Vine featured the M train at a subway stop in New York City. Over time, there was more competition for eyeballs and Vine creators began getting serious about their work. If you look at a list of the most watched Vine creators (*Tubular Labs*: February 2016), you will find that nine of the top ten are in either the Comedy category or the Sports category. At the top of the list is Thomas Sanders, a young man from Central Florida, with 284 million views in February. Sitting at number two with 255 million views is *BuzzFeed*, the popular social news service.

Vine Rules

You are supposed to be 13 years old to join Vine, according to the company's rules, but there are plenty of kids even younger who are actively consuming and creating videos using the app. *Common Sense Media* says Vine is best for teens who are ages 15 and older. As they explain on their site, "Many of the videos are harmless, but parents need to be aware that Vine is full of content that is inappropriate for children. With the most basic creative searching, kids can find nudity, sex, drug use, offensive language, and more."

Vine is available for iOS, Android, and Windows devices. In the Apple App Store, the app is listed for kids who are 17+. Again, these are guidelines that are rarely followed. Vine does have a set of rules posted on its website (**vine.co/rules**) that details Content Boundaries and use of Vine along with Spam and Abuse. There is little in terms of how to protect your privacy and manage your security, but they do include these four bullets that are worth noting.

Sensitive Media: Sensitive media, such as nudity or mild violence, may be subject to certain limitations, including but not limited to, warnings to users and restrictions preventing that content from appearing in Vine Channels.

Explicit Graphic Content: You may not publish or post explicit violent or otherwise graphic content, such as explicit depictions of child abuse, animal abuse, or bodily harm.

Pornography and Sexually Explicit Content: You may not post content that is pornographic or sexually explicit — even if it is of yourself or marked as sensitive.

Threats: You may not publish or post content that is intended to incite others to commit violence, mocks victims of violence, or includes a direct and specific threat of violence to others.

If we had to outline three additional things that parents need to know about Vine, they include:

Peer pressure: There is no shortage of pressure to do everything from engaging in trending stunts, which we talked about earlier in the book, to sharing inappropriate videos. Again, especially among teens, the attention they receive on social media is one of the primary ways that they determine their self-worth. If a Vine is going to get more likes, they are willing to take more risks.

Direct messaging: In the spring of 2014, Vine released direct messages. This lets friends send videos or messages to each other privately. The worrisome aspect is that you can send and receive both video and text messages from people who aren't your friends on Vine (keep in mind there are more than 40 million users on the service, making it a massive community automatically filled with a world of strangers).

Vine Kids: Early in 2015, Vine took a big step to make parents feel more comfortable with their service. They launched an iOS app called Vine Kids, which is available for preschoolers and young preteens. These videos are all pre-selected so that there is no inappropriate content. In short, this download is mostly filled with cute animated characters and quirky sounds.

Vine Opportunities

More and more you will hear stories about independent Vine creators who are making a living creating short videos and skits. Most often, these individuals will work with brands who are looking to attach themselves to influential personalities online. While many are adults, some are teens. One unique story includes a family from Stratford, Ontario. Dad Stewart Reynolds, his wife Shannon, and their boys Gregor (14) and Owen (17) make daily appearances on Vine. Stewart (AKA @Brittlestar) is closing in on one million followers. Both boys also have significant followings on Vine and other social media services.

Stewart has turned his video-making passion into a business for the entire family. Nonetheless, he's still careful about how his kids share online. "The safety of my kids is always paramount, obviously, but that said I always want to make sure that the content they're creating is the content they want to create and isn't going to make them hugely embarrassed in the future," he explains. "Make no mistake, everyone is embarrassed when they look back and see themselves as kids, but this new generations' lives have been hyper-documented. The effect being that the Internet is forever, so be aware of that... however, everyone their age will have something embarrassing online. The trick is to help your kids have as few SUPER embarrassing (read: possibly damaging) content pieces out there."

He goes on to explain how creating social video is what the family does to pay the bills. He also admits that, thanks to Vine, he gets to spend more time with his teenage kids than most families. It's the cool factor when Dad is a big deal online! Whether you sign on to Vine and start making videos or simply observe and monitor from afar, take the time to thoroughly understand the communities where your kids are spending the most time.

Live Streaming Video Services

At the South by Southwest (SXSW) Conference and Festival in March 2015, journalist Dan Rather sat on stage talking with a moderator about the future of new media. Throughout the audience, bloggers and tech enthusiasts listened carefully to the icon explain that, when it comes to technology and the news, humans were moving much more quickly than organizations ever could. Although his session was called "Breaking the News in the Age of Snapchat," every row in the audience had at least one person who was live streaming the session from their smartphone so that anyone beyond the four walls of the conference room could follow along.

Every year at this particular news media event, there is one star service that steals the show. In 2015, it was Meerkat. The little app with the odd name dominated headlines. Everywhere you went at SXSW, people were holding up smartphones and streaming everything that landed in front of them. During the days following SXSW, it looked as though this independent company had a solid chance to dominate the shiny new live-streaming market. However, after just a couple of weeks, Twitter subsequently launched a competitor called Periscope.

By December of that same year, Periscope was named Apple's iPhone App of the Year. This was the tool, many said, that was going to change the future of how we watch. Using this download is pretty simple, yet perhaps dangerously so. Once you download Periscope on your iPhone or Android device, you simply click on the red icon in the bottom right corner of the screen. Describe (in text) what you're going to stream, share it on Twitter, and you are good to go.

What used to take news organizations hours to do and cost them thousands of dollars, is now easy and free. Of course the quality of what's regularly streaming isn't in the ballpark of mainstream media, but it certainly has potential to disrupt what content we consume.

While it looked as though Periscope had taken over the top spot in the live-streaming race, Facebook and YouTube are now working hard to make a mark in this space. In fact, Facebook recently made some significant enhancements to its service. Initially, Facebook Live was only available to public personalities, but today it's available to most users.

Like all things Zuckerberg, they're also quick to add new features and functionality. They now make it easy to go live in Facebook Groups & Events, so you can engage your community. They've also added live reactions, replay comments, and live filters. If you think of this visually, it means that while you're streaming live video you will instantly see your viewers' reactions. Finally, they are tying your live broadcast to your location. With the Facebook Live Map, it's easy to watch people in dozens of countries who are broadcasting at any given moment.

Live Streaming Concerns

In a *TeenSafe.com* article, it talks about an ABC News investigation that focuses on some of the concerns with these apps. They include the following bullets, on which we've expounded below:

Real-time cyberbullying: As soon as your child goes live, there can easily be someone watching–and commenting–in inappropriate ways. Unlike traditional news, there is no way to protect the broadcaster from seeing this information since all of these apps are set up so that you are watching what people are saying (using the front-facing camera view is the most common). This makes it difficult to protect your children because everything is happening in real-time and, in some cases, the video isn't always available after the broadcast. For example, Facebook will store the video indefinitely (unless you delete it), but Periscope will remove the video after 24 hours.

Sexual harassment: With so many ways to reach young people online, live streaming opens up a frightening world. A simple broadcast from a child's bedroom can get inappropriate quickly if a friend or stranger starts to dare that individual to do something sexual in front of the camera. It's easy for the young broadcaster to underestimate the potential reach of this stream. While she may feel comfortable in her own home, it's plausible that she gets thousands of viewers from her town, state, country, and well beyond.

Location services: Since these companies want to tie each broadcast to a specific location, this presents a significant problem from both a privacy and security standpoint. While creating a YouTube video requires time to shoot and edit, meaning your child may notice he or she inadvertently shared his or her address when recording in front of a house, there is no way to take back a moment on a live stream. That means that everything that happens around you could identify your location.

Live Streaming Monitoring

For parents who did not grow up with social media while in school, it's easy to imagine how harmful the full functionality of these apps can be if they're not used responsibly. One private moment can be shared live with anyone online (whether you're broadcasting or being broadcasted). One simple stream can also easily identify your exact location. In Periscope, for example, if you click on the earth icon at the top of the screen you can zoom in to see where people are broadcasting in very specific neighborhoods. Here are three quick things parents can do to keep kids safe on live streaming services:

Turn off location settings: Teach your child to turn off location services on all of these apps. While they may see some compelling reason to turn on location services, it's a first and important step to protect their privacy and security.

Download live streaming apps: It is worth downloading the most popular live streaming apps, such as Meerkat and Periscope. Also, monitor what your child is streaming on Facebook Live. Another app worth downloading is YouKnow, which works on smartphones and on computers. In a recent *FamilyCircle.com* article, they mention a disturbing trend where kids leave this service streaming live all night and tag these streams #sleepingsquad.

Research new streaming services: It is increasingly tough to stay on top of the latest technology, especially since this category of apps and services is absolutely exploding. For example, Twitch.tv now has about 100 million unique visitors every single month. It initially launched as a place where gamers streamed their gameplay, but it's expanded well beyond this category. The Amazon-owned company recently streamed 201 episodes of Julia Child's "The French Chef" on its food channel. In short, read tech blogs such as *Mashable* and *Techcrunch* to keep in the loop on the latest launches.

While live streaming is still in its infancy, Facebook is charging ahead and will inevitably take over as the star of the show. Take time to learn more about this space, so you can be in the know about the various concerns and benefits.

How do I find videos associated with my child?

Many parents mistakenly believe that searching YouTube will present any videos available online that may be of personal interest regarding their children. While YouTube is one of the largest video repositories, it is not the only place that you should look. Many children know that their parents are aware of YouTube, and seek lesser-known services that may escape parental detection. These include popular websites such as Vine, Facebook, Vimeo, LiveLeak, and UStream. There are several dozen video services that could contain valuable content, and searching each can be extremely tedious. Fortunately, Google and Bing have simplified the process for you.

Google Videos at **video.google.com** provides a search engine that displays only online videos. It searches all of the most popular services as well as those of which you may not be aware. As an example, a search on YouTube for "school bus fight" returned over 342,000 results. However, this same search on Google Videos returned over 3 million results. These include the results identified in the previous YouTube search plus any videos from other sites, such as Vine, that meet the search criteria. This will often lead to duplicate videos that have been posted by news websites and social networks. Parents can enter any relevant search terms into this engine to filter millions of video results into a digestible amount. Your terms may include your child's name, user names, school, or sports team.

A search of "school bus fight Toronto" produced 709 videos at the time of this writing. Most of these were amateur videos captured with cellular phones over the past decade. This can present quite a needle in a haystack for parents trying to find relevant videos after a recent incident. We suggest using Google's "Search Tools" visible directly below every search field. Clicking this button presents several new search filters including the "Time" option. This feature allows you to filter results by time range including the past 24 hours, week, month, or year. Figure 5.01 displays this menu in use.

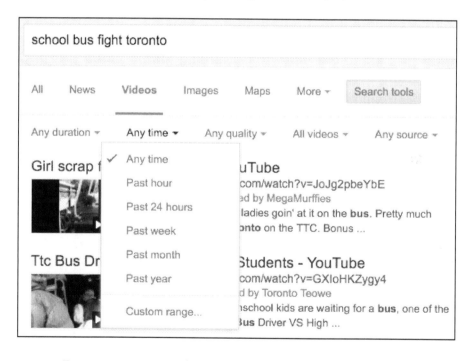

Figure 5.01: A Google Videos search with advanced filters.

Google is not the only valuable provider for this type of service. One feature that makes Bing a favorite site for searching videos is the instant video playback option. When viewing a video search results page at **video.bing.com**, simply hovering the cursor over the video still shot will start the video playback from the beginning of the video. This eliminates the need to navigate to each video page for playback to determine the value of the video. Whether using Google or Bing to locate videos, we recommend turning off the "safe search" feature. This feature is designed to prohibit some videos with adult content from displaying. With concerns related to children, it is often these types of videos that are desired by parents.

After you have searched Google Videos and Bing Videos for keywords associated with your child, you might find many video pages that need to be researched. Visiting each will present individual videos that can be easily played, paused, and repeated. We believe that the visual content is only a small portion of the most interesting content. Most video pages allow comments below the video. Anyone can post new messages or respond to existing comments. This area is often more interesting to curious parents. The details presented here will likely provide more context to concerning situations than a brief video.

As an example, we located a video during our previous search concerning school bus fights in Toronto. The brief video was poor quality and provided very little information about the incident. In the comments area below the video, over 142 messages provided much more context. Conversations between the children that were present during the incident quickly revealed the history between the students being attacked and the provokers. Most concerning were the discussions announcing upcoming revenge for the attack and promises of more future violence. Most of the user profiles posting this incriminating content clearly identified students by real name and photos. Clicking on any user name directly before the message presented complete profiles including additional videos that were uploaded or watched by each participant in the fight. Law enforcement has been using this information during investigations for years. We believe it is time that parents become more involved in finding this content.

Michael's Hacks

How do I find additional copies of videos?

Because online videos are often presented with user comments and conversations, parents should locate every copy of any videos of interest. These duplicates may contain additional dialogue from online viewers that could provide additional context to the situation surrounding the video. There was an explanation earlier of conducting a reverse image search on the profile image of your child's account. This technique has proven to be extremely valuable when searching for duplicate images of your child. You will likely locate new content associated with him or her that would otherwise have never been found. Many parents desire to replicate that method for videos.

While there is no official reverse video search option, applying the techniques to still captures of videos can provide amazing results. You can now conduct reverse image searches on videos from Vimeo, Facebook, Vine, Liveleak, Backpage, and others. As the popularity of online videos is catching up to images, you must always consider reverse video searches. They will identify additional websites hosting the target videos of interest. Before explaining the techniques, consider the reasons why you may want to conduct this type of activity.

School administrative personnel are constantly notified of inappropriate video material being posted online. Identifying these videos consisting of fights, malicious plans, and bullying, may be enough to take care of the situation. However, identifying the numerous copies on other websites will help adults understand the magnitude of the situation.

Parents may be aware of their child's video page on YouTube, but might be oblivious to a lesser-known profile on the video service Vimeo. Children will often post more incriminating videos through avenues that are less likely to be monitored by adults. If a child posts a video from his or her YouTube page on the Vimeo page, you can now connect the two accounts and analyze the content. Instead of an extremely technical and complicated overview of how images from videos are available within the source code of video pages, we share a custom reverse video search tool that will automate the entire process easily at **inteltechniques.com/OSINT/reverse.video.html**.

Similar to the previous search tools that we have explained, this page will automate a specific task. This page includes a search field that awaits a YouTube, Vimeo, Facebook, Vine, Instagram, or LiveLeak video ID (Figure 5.02). When executed, several new tabs will open with your reverse image searches for that video from Google, Bing, TinEye, Yandex, and Baidu. The final option allows you to enter the entire URL of any image that you locate and the reverse image process is conducted. Many parents rely on this tool almost every day, and we hope that you will also find it beneficial.

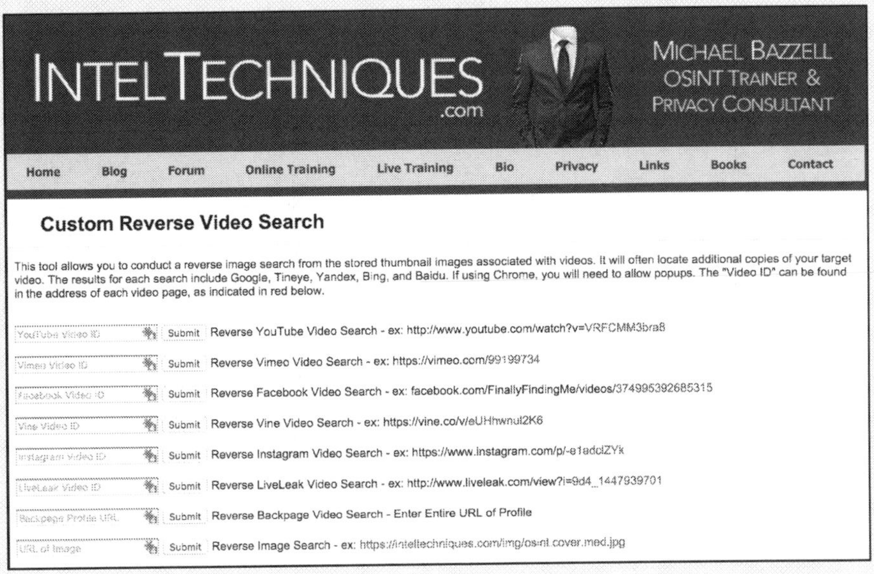

Figure 5.02: The IntelTechniques Custom Reverse Video Search Tool.

These sources are not the only video-sharing services on the Internet. Wikipedia identifies dozens of these sites, but searching each of them can become tedious. These sites are no longer restricted to pages of video files with standard extensions such as mp4, mpg, and flv. Today, services such as Instagram and Vine allow embedded videos that do not conform to yesterday's video standards. Many new services present the viewer with animated GIF files that only appear as true videos. Fortunately, search engines like Google and Bing offer a search across all of the types.

What if I can't play the videos?

The vast majority of videos located by parents will be publicly visible and will begin playing as soon as the pages are opened. Some privacy and security settings within the video services allow restrictions that can be frustrating to parents. While some private videos will be impossible to circumvent, we have a couple of methods that will assist in unlocking the content.

Several YouTube videos have been tagged as violent, sexual, or otherwise inappropriate for young viewers. Many demand that you log into a Google account and verify your date of birth in order to view the content. Most parents prefer to not be logged into any personal account while researching their children. Any time you are searching through a Google product while logged into an account, you take the risk of exposing your presence with accidental clicks that might announce your interest. One easy technique should remove this restriction. As an example, navigate to the following website and notice the inability to view the video. If you are not logged into a Google account with a verified age, you should see a warning about mature content. This video cannot be played by the everyday web visitor. Please be warned that the content in this example contains very disturbing video, hence the blockage by YouTube.

https://www.youtube.com/watch?v=SZqNKAd_gTw

In this example, the YouTube Video ID is "SZqNKAd_gTw." In order to view this video through YouTube without a third party service, and without supplying the credentials for your personal Google account, you can generate the following URL. Replace "SZqNKAd_gTw" with the ID of your child's video. The result will be the restricted video in full screen view.

https://www.youtube.com/v/SZqNKAd_gTw

How do I download a video associated with my child?

If you locate disturbing video relevant to your child, you will likely want to obtain an offline copy. This could be to preserve and document the activity for later discussion. The video within the online website could disappear at any time. We always recommend downloading interesting videos right away. YouTube and other services do not offer a native ability to download content. To do this, you will need to use a third party service. While you are watching any YouTube video, you can add the letters "PWN" to the beginning of the address in order to download the video to your computer. To test this, navigate to the following website.

http://www.youtube.com/watch?v=OmZyrynlk2w

Now, add "PWN" to the beginning, as indicated in the following address.

http://www.pwnyoutube.com/watch?v= OmZyrynlk2w

You will be presented a new page with many options including the ability to download the video, download only the audio, convert the video to a different format, and bypass the age restriction as discussed earlier.

Summary

Like any emerging media, there are positives and negatives. Today, we are perfectly set up to consume and create content on dozens of mobile devices. For kids, this is perhaps too much choice. It used to be simple for parents to control what kids watched on television. They could just turn off the TV, or do what many moms and dads did, threaten to cancel the cable. Today, it's unrealistic to assume that parents can have that same type of control, especially when a child enters the teen years. However, it is possible to take a bit of that control back from your children, especially as we look to the future.

According to Ooyala, video consumption on tablets and smartphones has grown 170 percent since 2013. When it comes to the mobile-first generation, 69 percent of videos watched were less than ten minutes long. While Vine is just one of the micro video apps we discussed earlier, there will be plenty more in the years to come that will capitalize on this trend of bite-sized, playful (and yes, often inappropriate) content.

While you may be worrying about your child texting, you now know it's also especially important to focus on visual social media–both images and video. We showed you how to find where your kids may be featured in videos online. You should now also have a solid understanding of other forms of online video, whether your child is sharing six-second clips or streaming all night long. In the next chapter, we will look at mobile apps that your kids are probably using right now. From ephemeral messaging to casual dating, we will demystify how these tools work and inform you of strategies you need to know to keep your kids safe when using them.

Chapter Six
Mobile Apps

If you browse through journalist Stuart Dredge's top ten children's app trends for 2015, you will see some encouraging highlights. From digital storytelling to kids coding to musical creation, there are plenty of reasons that parents should support mobile technology. In fact, in some cases, it's actually good for kids. He also explains in his article on *TheGuardian.com* that this support should be in combination with other activities.

"YES, kids should be reading books, riding bikes, playing sports, drawing pictures with pencils, digging for worms... doing things away from screens. Using apps shouldn't replace all that, and it's a parental responsibility to make sure that it doesn't."

ScratchJr is just one example of a download that is both educational and entertaining, the perfect formula to entice preschoolers and even young preteens. Developed through a collaboration of a number of organizations such as the Lifelong Kindergarten Research Group and the MIT Media Lab, the app is made for kids ages five to seven and teaches many important lessons for young developers. With simple graphical blocks, children prompt cute characters to dance and sing against scenic backgrounds. Throughout the process, they are learning the very basics of coding, an important skill in today's wired world.

In fact, there are hundreds of excellent apps to teach your children spelling, math, music, and much more. Companies such as SagoSago and TocaBoca make some of the best downloads for preschoolers. With dozens of award-winning titles, they create go-to apps that parents will love. As they explain on their site, "We make digital toys that help stimulate the imagination, and that you can play together with your kids. Best of all—we do it in a safe way without advertising or in-app purchases." That means moms and dads can rest easy when their littlest family members are immersed in this software.

As kids grow up, the altruistic nature of developers creating for them seems to disappear. Instead, the most popular downloads for teens focus on that group's tech wants, which is worrisome to parents. For starters, three of the biggest trends we're seeing right now in this space are the rise of anonymous apps, location-based apps, and ephemeral messaging. Within all of these categories there is cause for concern.

For starters, anonymous apps tend to lead to bullying. Within this category there are services such as Whisper. This app lets users post secret confessions along with background images. At any given moment, looking through the messages within this app will make any parent squirm. Nonetheless, more than 20 million people use this service on a regular basis. Another app that lives in this category is Yik Yak. We will review both below so parents understand the risks associated with them and how you can easily locate your kids when they're using them.

We will also address location-based technology in the context of dating apps. While you may think that services such as Tinder are populated exclusively with adults looking to hook up, a *TeenVogue.com* article states that 2.5 percent of the app's users are ages 13 to 17. Although Tinder only matches daters in this age range with other kids in this age range, it's easy enough for anyone to lie about their age when signing up for this service. This means in one swipe, your child is talking–and even worse–planning to meet a stranger.

Snapchat

We should first detail the basics of ephemeral messaging. This is content that disappears after another person views it. Snapchat is one example of a popular service in this category. According to a Piper Jaffray survey, 19 percent of teens say Snapchat is the most important social network. The app also boasts about 4 billion video views a day, matching what people are watching on Facebook.

Snapchat is a mobile app, available for iOS and Android devices, which lets you share messages, photos, videos, and more. It's an understatement to say that it is probably one of the more clumsy social networks in terms of user experience. In other words, it will take a savvy Snapchatter (yes, that's the official term) to show you how to find your way around here. As social media marketer Gary Vaynerchuk explains in a blog post on his site, it's actually not clumsy but instead just mirroring reality.

"I was surprised early on that people didn't realize that the way Snapchat works is much closer to how we communicate face to face than any other social network. What I mean by this is that: when we talk to each other, passing in the halls or just living out our lives, those moments disappear. Snapchat emulates that behavior and psychology."

Snapchat Home: When you first open the app, the ghost icon at the top middle part of the screen is your way Home (this is also called your profile page). This is where you will find how many people have added you, add friends, and see a list of your friends. If you swipe up from there, you can then take a photo or shoot a short video. Once you're done, you use one of the three icons at the top right to add emojis, add text, and doodles. From this point, you can send that snap to friends using the arrow on the bottom right. You can also add this to your Snapchat Story using the box with the plus sign, which is a real-time feed that expires after 24 hours. Finally, you can also use the arrow and line icon to save your creation to your phone.

Snapchat Stories: If you go back to your Home screen (remember, the ghost icon), you can then swipe right to see these features in this order. First up are Stories, including My Story at the top of the page. You can click on the three vertical dots to see each snap in your story and click on the snap to unveil the delete button if you want to get rid of it. Other stories from people you follow are under Recent Updates. The general purpose of My Story is to give friends insight into moments in your life. Very often, it is here where teens share too much, and could compromise their privacy and security.

Snapchat Discover: In this section, which you can reveal with a swipe right from Snapchat Stories, you will see a number of well-known publishers that create their own multimedia stories. According to *Digiday*, *Cosmopolitan* gets 3 million readers a day here. These brands pay for this presence. In 2014, the company's founder made headlines when he announced that businesses would pay at least $750,000 a day to advertise on his app.

Snapchat Messages: If you go back Home (the ghost icon), swipe up and left to see your activity feed. This includes your messages and a list of people who have added you. From here, you can also swipe right on a friend's name to send them a chat (which will eventually disappear after they view it).

Snapchat Filters: This is probably one of the more interesting parts of the app. Within filters, you can change the look of your image or video. With Geofilters, you can add images that are tied to your specific location. For example, if you're in New York City and swipe up on your snap, you will see New York City (and other filters) that you can easily add. To turn filters on, go back to your Home screen (the ghost icon) and click on the Settings icon in the top right corner. From here, you can turn on filters, enable travel mode to reduce mobile data on the go, and manage permissions. It's here that you can manage who can send snaps and view your story. In other words, for parents teaching kids about Snapchat, getting acquainted with Snapchat Settings is key. Note: If you want to add one of Snapchat's selfie filters, so you can shoot rainbows out of your mouth and more, simply use the front-facing camera to take a selfie and then hold your finger on your face to bring up the grid; at this point, you will be able to add these goofy filters.

About Snapchatters

In the United States, this is the breakdown of Snapchat's youngest users—23 percent of them are between the ages of 13 and 17. In the company's own words, the wider range of users are mainly 13- to 34-year-olds who love Snapchat for three main reasons:

Get Perspective: Snaps provide a personal window into the way you and your friends see the world.

Be Here, Now: Stories are updated in real-time and expire after 24 hours.

Express Yourself: Snaps are a reflection of who you are in the moment—there is no need to curate an everlasting persona.

Here is some information on commonly used words on Snapchat:

Snapcode: On your Home screen, this is the unique yellow scannable code with your image in the centre. Friends can scan this code to add you on Snapchat.

Snapcash: When a Snapchatter has added their debit card in the app (thanks to mobile payment software Square), they can send money to other Snapchatters on their contact list who have this same feature enabled. This is only available in the United States and participants must be older than 18.

Trophies: This is where Snapchat gamifies your social experience. The more you use the app, the more trophies you can unlock. Click on the trophy icon on your Home screen to find out how well you're doing on this front.

Chat 2.0: A new feature on Snapchat is Chat 2.0, which lets users send text chats, but also lets them send video chats and make voice calls. For video chats, a friend can just watch to see you, but they are not forced to engage in the video portion of the conversation (they can simply send audio). Through Voice Calls, users can have audio conversations and send messages. It's a bit complicated to explain; this is how *Techcrunch* describes Chat 2.0:

"It lets private conversations morph between mediums depending on what users want to show or tell, and whether they can speak up or must stay silent. As WhatsApp focuses on simplicity and Facebook Messenger chases commerce, Snapchat is positioning itself as the most vivid, human way to chat."

Snapchat Safety Center

This resource on Snapchat's site is fairly comprehensive and located at **snapchat.com/safety**. Within it you will find a link to the Snapchat Safety Guide for Parents & Teachers. This PDF download includes much of the information we mention above, but it also details a few other points that are worth noting. It has important steps to teach parents how to block a user, report abuse, and delete an account, which we describe below.

Block a User: On your Home screen, go to My Friends and locate someone whom you would like to block. When you tap on their profile, select the gear icon to block the user. This will stop the blocked user from sending you snaps or chats, and that user will not be able to see your Story. Depending on your relationship with the person you want to block, you may need to take additional steps to complete this process. Reading through Snapchat's guide to blocking will provide you with all of the details for this process.

Report Abuse: If there are ongoing issues with someone harassing your child on Snapchat, you can send an email to safety@snapchat.com. You can also get help from the Support section on the site.

Delete an Account: If for some reason you want to delete an account entirely, visit Snapchat's account deletion option located on their website at https://accounts.snapchat.com/accounts/delete_account. It will help you remove a Snapchat account, as long as you have the user name and password. If you do not have this information, check out this handy PDF that makes it easy to request that Snapchat deletes your minor's account: https://www.snapchat.com/static_files/deletion_request.pdf.

We could probably write an entire book about Snapchat safety. The company is experiencing phenomenal growth, which means they are also rapidly releasing new features to keep up with the competition (mainly Facebook!). As a result, it's difficult for parents to stay on top of how this app works. The best recommendation we can give you in terms of monitoring your kids on Snapchat is to use the information we provide above to get your own account up and running. When you understand how this app works, it will be easier to educate your child.

Musical.ly

Every six months or so, kids tend to discover a new app that they make all the rage. While Snapchat continues to be a go-to download for children of all ages (try to find a 6-year-old who hasn't used Snapchat's Face Swap feature), musical.ly is rising up in popularity with a reported 60 million users. Like its name, this app is all about creating music. Primarily, users choose from an all-hits library of 15-second tracks and lip sync over them. There is also an option to create your own music videos. Sure, it sounds innocent enough, but for your youngest kids at home (including preschoolers and preteens), this app includes a wide range of inappropriate content such as an abundance of overly sexual songs. These inevitably lead to some pretty sexually charged videos and bad language.

Common Sense Media gives this app a rating of 16+, but chances are you will have a hard time keeping your young teens away from it. As we've mentioned before, make it a habit to download apps that your kids are trying so that you understand how they function. You can also check out musical.ly on Instagram to get a preview of the types of videos kids are making. Aside from lip syncing, the app leverages other popular digital trends, such as the ability to add filters, share on social media, and save videos to your camera roll. Like many new social networks, likes are also part of its appeal. Within the musical.ly community you can see how your videos are ranking.

This isn't just an app for small groups of friends. Within the settings you can make your account private or public. There is also a messaging component, so some kids may experience bullying from other users. Also, according to the company's privacy policy, they collect information about your location if you give them permission. On the topic of location, here are a few more strategies to understand how location-based tools affect your child's safety and security.

Location-based Chatting

Children have been using some form of online chat since the late nineties when Yahoo! Messenger was the standard way of communicating. A lot has changed since then. Today, kids embrace advanced technologies, such as geolocation, to enhance their communication experiences. Since every smartphone has a GPS receiver inside, it is common for children to announce their location and seek out others within their proximity. This is a very fun and amazing way to participate in a new social space. It can also be very dangerous. First, let's take a look at location-based messaging.

Yik Yak (**www.yikyak.com**) is a social media smartphone application. It is available for iOS and Android and it allows people to create and view discussion threads within a 5-mile radius. It is intended for sharing primarily with those in proximity to the user, making it intimate and relevant for people reading the posts. All users have the ability to contribute to the message stream by writing, responding, and "voting up" or "voting down" (liking or disliking) each post. This app quickly became a huge headache for schools across North America.

Because Yik Yak users are anonymous, it presents an avenue for bullying and threats of violence. Children began immediately posting threatening content directed toward victims within the boundaries of the school. Other children would follow the posts as they were also within the boundaries. From a playground, children were creating an extremely toxic environment within a social space where they were unsupervised. Eventually, school administrators started noticing and began to take action. In 2014, Yik Yak began implementing rules that banned the use of the service within the boundaries of middle and high schools. This helped, but has not solved the problem.

Today, children still flock to Yik Yak and continue to harass, threaten, and bully their victims. While they cannot do this at school, they can still access the app at malls, restaurants, and any other place that children tend to visit. While Yik Yak is very popular, it is not the only option. Other location-based message apps, such as Whisper (**whisper.sh**) and Nearby (**wnmlive.com**), are gaining in popularity. We have found that the app most popular in your area will vary from those apps popular in other locations. Parents should identify the services being used by the children close to them.

How do I use these apps?

The previous methods of locating social network content about your child involved opening a web browser and digging around. Apps are a different story. In order to investigate the use of application-based services, you will need to install the apps on your device. We know of many parents who keep a secondary Wi-Fi-only smartphone or tablet just for this purpose. It prevents the abundance of apps from crowding or impacting their real-world devices. Affordable entry-level tablets can be found online for well under $100. These will also provide a larger screen than your smartphone. The downside to this is that you will not have cellular service, which will be required for some of the methods presented in a moment.

If you have an Android device, you will want to visit the Play Store app and search for any desired app. Apple users will do this in the App Store. The installation should be effortless. Some apps will require you to create an account while others will function without configuration. We encourage you to obtain and familiarize yourself with any apps that you believe your children could be using. Converting your smartphone or dedicated gadget into an app-monitoring device will prepare you for the next suggestions.

After you have installed your desired apps, you are ready to attempt to locate your children within them. Regarding Yik Yak, Whisper, and Nearby, you must be physically near your child in order to see any posts that could be originating from his or her device. At a minimum, this can be a few miles. A perfect time for this would be when your child is in his or her room with friends and you are also in the house. Alternatively, you could monitor any nearby communications from your vehicle as you wait for your child outside of a party or social event.

Location-based Dating

Many parents reading this will remember a time when young people mingled in person and dated people who they met through these interactions. Today, most young people meet through social networks and dating apps. While this can result in innocent relationships, it is ripe for abuse by online predators. The dating websites of yesterday are being replaced with location-based apps today. These smartphone programs identify the location of the user, compare it to a database of other nearby users, and allow the opportunity to immediately meet someone who is nearby. One of the most popular dating apps is Tinder.

Tinder is very simple and easy to use. It finds your child's location using GPS, then uses his or her Facebook information to create a profile. A Tinder profile is made up of your child's first name, age, photos and any Facebook "Likes." Recently, Tinder also added a feature that lets your child share education and occupation information. This can expose sensitive details such as the school attended. Tinder then finds potential matches near your child and presents them on the screen including a photo of the potential partner. This can be filtered by age and distance, as many predators do, to find nearby young adults. Your child can swipe each result, right to "like" them or left to "pass." If any "likes" also liked your child, it is considered a match and they can start instant messaging.

Tinder is not the only prominent location-based dating app popular with kids. Other offerings such as Blendr, Skout, Anonymous Dating, Sex Only, Grindr, Badoo, and MeetMe are common with numerous schools internationally. Our recommendations to parents are two-fold. First, identify the dating apps popular with your child and his or her peers. This could be obtained through a conversation, or by viewing the contents of a smartphone. Next, install and execute the appropriate apps on your own device in order to identify any concerns.

How do I find my child on location-based dating apps?

After you have installed the apps of interest on your own device, you should make sure that you are physically within one mile of your child. Open each dating app and log into the service. Make sure that your GPS is enabled. When prompted, identify yourself as the gender of your child's romantic interest and choose the appropriate age range. All of these apps require users to be at least 18 years of age; however, many children will lie about this. Selecting 18 as an age preference will likely suffice for your search needs. Look through all of the results. If you identify your child's profile, take note of any information that you can glean from it.

If you have located your child within an online dating app, we can assure you of two things. Your child is receiving sexual solicitations from predators, and the risk of attack has substantially increased. In Chapter Eight, we will explain how pedophiles use these apps as avenues into the lives of children. In Chapter Nine, we present solutions for proper reporting of inappropriate behavior.

What about messaging apps such as Kik?

There are now an abundance of text messaging applications that children use instead of traditional text messaging through a cellular provider. While Kik is one of the most popular, other options such as WhatsApp, Viber, and ReTXT are gaining many new users internationally. Determining the app that your child uses will likely require a conversation or some snooping. Unfortunately for parents, there is no way of searching the Internet for content posted within Kik by your child. Your only option would be to view the messages directly from the device used. However, knowing which apps are popular in your child's school will give you an advantage during Internet safety conversations with him or her. Just knowing that a parent is aware of the usage might present a deterrent to the child using the apps.

Summary

Within this chapter we've discussed how mobile apps work and which mobile apps are getting the most attention on your child's phone. For parents of preschoolers and preteens, now is the time to build a relationship with your kids in terms of app guidance. It is possible during these years to teach children about safe app usage. Whether it's explaining to them why they should avoid in-app purchases or reminding them to choose smart passwords (more on this later), it's never too soon to start this conversation.

When your child enters their teen years, it's advantageous to get a good handle on what apps are rising in popularity within their peer group. We've mentioned *Common Sense Media* in the past, which is a great resource to learn about which apps are suitable for kids of all ages. It's also worth reading popular tech blogs, such as *Mashable*, to keep on top of this ever-changing information. As you discover where your teen is spending the most in-app time, download these same apps on your phone and take a few minutes each day (whether it's at breakfast or in front the television) to acquaint yourself with how they work. It will be virtually impossible to have a meaningful conversation with your child about how they're using these app-based social networks if you don't understand the first thing about how they work. In the next section, we'll dig further into how to manage your child's screen time. We will outline screen time risks for preschoolers, preteens, and teens and strategies to manage Internet usage effectively. We will also discuss must-have monitoring tools and security tips.

A Question from a Parent

Jill Lewis: How do we teach our kids not to trust strangers online without making them paranoid? When my daughter was 10, I thought she was on a kid friendly site with her friend but then later that night I got a call from her principal as the girls had landed on a Russian dating website.

Amber's Answer: There is a good chance that no amount of warning will make your child too paranoid. In fact, it is entirely beneficial if your child is fearful of strangers online. Often times young people are less afraid of people they don't know on the Internet because there is a perceived intimacy with that person; after all, social media networks have redefined the definition of a friend to include people you don't know face to face. Although your daughter is only 10 years old, we know that many kids in this age group are currently active on social media sites, such as Instagram. Without going into many details, there are plenty of examples of predators who are targeting preteens through these popular services. While you don't want to scare your daughter off the Internet entirely, it's a good idea to have conversations to determine new sites she's visiting and together work out if they are appropriate. If you revisit this topic on a regular basis, and address the stranger danger issue every time, you will be in a better position to properly deal with any potential issues since there is open dialogue. On the flip side, being confrontational when you find out that there is an issue with someone she doesn't know online will only drive her further away.

Chapter Seven
Screen Time

While we've addressed what our kids are doing on certain platforms, such as Facebook, Twitter, Instagram, and more, we haven't explored how these new ways of communicating are having an impact on their lives. We are facing a flurry of reports about how screen time is affecting today's kids. As we mentioned, one of the main problems with standards from parent groups is that their research is often outdated, not addressing the reality that we live in today. After all, it's difficult to adopt guidelines that are 5 years old if your child is using technology and apps that just launched a few months ago. Again, we're adapting much more quickly than screen time standards. A quick Google search will lead to the following article headlines:

- Kids and Screen Time: What Does the Research Say?
- Pediatricians Rethink Screen Time Policy for Children
- How Much Screen Time is OK for My Kids?

Yes, for the most part, even page one of Google search results leads to more confusion, filling parents' minds with unanswered questions about what's appropriate and what's not. Unfortunately, there isn't one magic bullet to solve this screen time dilemma. Perhaps the most helpful (and balanced) advice we have seen is from Lisa Guernsey, author of *Screen Time: How Electronic Media–From Baby Videos to Educational Software–Affects Your Young Child*. In her book she simplifies what you need to think about when it comes to your kids and their time online; she calls this "the three Cs."

Content

It's far too easy to forget that not all content is created equal. If your preschooler is watching cat videos on YouTube, that is not the same as your preschooler diving into the Avokiddo ABC Ride app (which encourages kids to use logic to find hidden letters and learn about the alphabet). If your preteen is playing Angry Birds, that is not the same as your preteen creating on GarageBand (where they can craft pro-like music recordings). If your teen is on Snapchat, that's not the same as your teen drawing on Autodesk Sketch (where they can design beautiful artwork).

Context

This is perhaps one of the most important elements to consider when your child spends time in front of a screen. Let's say, for example, that your kid spent most of his Saturday at a ball hockey tournament followed by a swimming competition followed by karate lessons. At this point your son has had a lot of physical activity. While you may have a household rule of no more than 30 minutes a day in front of a screen, on this day the context changes and perhaps an hour is OK.

Another example can include family travel. If you have a 16-hour road trip to Florida for spring break, you would probably be pretty happy if your 10-year-old daughter had a charged tablet en route to keep her entertained. In order to provide her with some tech guidance, before the trip you might visit *Common Sense Media* to download some educational apps for her to explore along the way. In this example, you are considering both content and context in terms of your screen time rules.

Finally, let's not forget those times when perhaps you are working from home and you need to do an important conference call. To keep your six-year-old son occupied, you might load up Toontastic–a fun and interactive cartoon-building and music app–so he can play along while you get a few moments of quiet to do business. In this case, the context changes because of your work.

Child

When you address each of your children as individuals in terms of determining their screen time limits, you will get closer to creating a manageable framework. For some kids, a little time on a device is a calming process–a few minutes to sit and relax. If you have a really active child, you might recommend that he watches videos online or she plays on apps as a form of downtime. If your child repeatedly cries when you pull her out of a game of Minecraft on the computer, you know there is a bigger problem that is potentially turning into an addiction.

Earlier in the book, we outlined some of the risks associated with too much screen time and your teens. We described yellow flags that include compulsive checking of devices, mood swings from elation to depression, and loss of interest in their old offline recreational activities. With younger children, the risks are perhaps more subtle. As Steven Gortmaker, professor of the practice of health sociology at Harvard says on *Harvard.edu*:

"Beyond the health effects, more than anything else when children are young, they need to spend time with real people: other children and adults. So we are very interested in helping parents lower the dose — not necessarily to ban technology, but just lower the dose so children don't spend their entire days with televisions, computers, video games, and now smartphones."

Based on this advice, parents must stay focused on monitoring how much time kids are spending online. With some careful attention, along with Guernsey's three Cs, moms and dads can work to figure out what's best for each child at home.

Some parents use tools such as an egg timer to establish screen time boundaries with young children. Others opt to create tech-free zones in the home, something pediatricians are starting to recommend more and more so there some places where gadgets are out of the picture. Finally, there are a number of new products that allow parents to have more control over Internet access in the house.

Circle is just one example of a product that can make this process more manageable. This cube-like piece of hardware, which sells for $99 US, works in conjunction with an app to help parents do the following:

- **Establish time limits**: Determine how much time each family member can spend per day online.
- **Go offline for bedtime**: Disconnect Internet access in the home when kids should all be in bed.
- **Set up safety filters**: Manage what content and platforms are appropriate depending on each child.
- **Pause button functionality**: Disable Internet access in the home for everyone at any given time.

With screen time, as parenting expert Alyson Schafer explains, establishing these boundaries at a young age is critical:

"The formative years are when children learn their expectations for how life works and how to behave. Hang up your coat when you come in the house, take your plate to the kitchen after dinner and so on. If this code of conduct is taught and enforced consistently, it becomes normative and automatic behavior. Kids raised this way just grab their plate when they get up not even thinking they are applying a rule. It's far harder to teach a 15-year-old that they must clean up after themselves if they never have before."

Next up, we will talk further about some best practices and screen time monitoring apps. Plus, we will address desktop and mobile security.

Best Practices

As we mention above, the most important screen time decision you can make is to help your children choose appropriate content. A quick LEGO search on YouTube can land your kid in front of some questionable videos. While it seems innocent enough, page one of "LEGO" search results will lead your child to the title LEGO ZOMBIES HARD RAIN.

The content consists of two men playing this first-person shooter game that lets you kill screaming zombies and bloody enemies. While your young daughter was on a quest to find cool ideas for her next LEGO project, she is now watching this video and getting exposed to some pretty violent content. What's even worse than the actual video are the comments attached, filled with bullying behavior and offensive language.

Incidentally, since YouTube is probably one the worst places for your kids to go in terms of easily stumbling upon content that is not family-friendly, Google has recently launched YouTube Kids. This app is available for iOS and Android devices. While it's not perfect in that the filtering system could let something inappropriate slip through (which you can easily flag), it does help your younger kids at home find content that they inherently want to watch—the fun shows and channels, such as Sesame Street, Stampylonghead, and more. There are also parental controls, so you can tailor the experience and control a built-in timer, and there are no ads.

While it all seems pretty dismal in terms of how easy it is for kids to land in an inappropriate place online, the good news is that there are plenty of websites and apps that are educational. It does take some digging to find them, but use a few main websites to get you started. Another favorite destination for parents is **www.coolmomtech.com**. Here you will find an entire section focused on the best apps for kids. In the educational section, there is a long list of titles that will help your children learn and explore. They also offer a weekly podcast if you prefer to listen to their advice (which extends beyond just tech). They have an in-depth Internet safety center that includes everything from when to buy your child a phone to reviews of new services such as SmartFeed, which is a subscription service to help manage a child's digital media diet.

Also, as *Common Sense Media* explains, there are really four main categories outlining different types of content that you should consider when making decisions about screen time.

- Passive consumption: watching TV, reading, and listening to music
- Interactive consumption: playing games and browsing the Internet
- Communication: video-chatting and using social media
- Content creation: using devices to make digital art or music

We have discussed three of these categories, but the one we didn't address in too much detail yet is Communication, in terms of video-chatting and email as learning aids. For many preschoolers, preteens, and teens, there are plenty of advantages in terms of encouraging them to use both of these tools to stay in touch with family members, such as cousins and grandparents. In fact, for the youngest of kids learning to read and write, email can be a fabulous tool to reinforce these skills and build their language comprehension confidence.

Maily, which is available for iOS and Android devices, is one such example. As *Fast Company* says in reference to the app, "Maily, a kids' email app for the iPad, is actually ahead of its time." This download is a handy tool for both preschoolers and young preteens. When kids get started, they can access creative message functionality to draw and take photos that they want to share. Parents are in charge in terms of approving content, so they can always see and approve all messages. There are also stamps (or stickers) so your child can have fun creating images for Grandma or Grandpa. Not only will your kids love this, their relatives will appreciate the fun-filled messages.

Tocomail for Gmail, which is available for iOS and Android devices, is an email app that is built just for teens. Since kids love to communicate using audio and video, these features are built into the app. Plus, children can create custom avatars for friends. This app also includes a safe list of contacts, a "Review" folder where kids can put emails that might need parent review, and much more. Perhaps your older teens will not want to use this download as they prefer to message on Facebook, Kik, or other services, however, for kids who are between 13 and 15 years old, this is a good bridge app in terms of teaching them positive messaging habits before they move on to other tools. It also helps to put parents in the middle of the relationship kids have with technology.

Here are a few other creative non-tech ideas to manage your child's screen time. Plus, we will dive into some helpful apps below to make this process easy and fun for the whole family.

Preschool: Enforce one hour between screen time and bedtime

While we've discussed the effects of technology in terms of helping young kids lead a healthy, social lifestyle, we have not yet discussed the effects of blue light. Children are drawn towards screens with their magical glow and bright content, but if screen time habits extend into the evening there are often sleep disturbances that can affect everyone in the home. As *eyesightonwellness.com* explains in terms of these risks:

"Among the leading risks of blue light exposure is it suppresses the release of melatonin, the hormone that tells us when it is time to sleep. An extended lack of deep sleep can in turn contribute to behavioral issues and weight gain due to overeating."

Also, the last thing you want as a parent of a kid who is in school is to struggle each morning to wake a tired child. The eye health site proceeds to describe that kids need at least one hour between screen time and bed time. Aside from problems sleeping, too much screen time can cause retinal stress (with the possibility of eye disease later in life). Incidentally, hardware manufacturers are starting to make changes in their device outputs to allow users to adjust blue light levels. For example, the latest version of iPhone software makes it easy to program for less blue light during nighttime hours (Apple calls this Night Shift mode), which you can enable by toggling on within Settings: Display & Brightness.

Preteen: Create a screen time reward system

While little kids might not be dependable in terms of completing their daily chores, preteens are well-equipped to do simple tasks such as cleaning their bedroom or tidying up the basement playroom. At this age, it's a good idea to begin explaining to your kids that you own the technology in the house and it's something you need to help them manage (not the other way around).

As always, there is technology that can help to facilitate this. A very popular app called ChoreMonster is a great tool for you and your preteens. In fact, *Parents Magazine* named it one of the must-have apps for families in 2015. Both parents and kids have access to the same account. For parents, you can create scheduled chores and approve them when they're done. You can add rewards to a child's point collection so they can, for example, get a certain amount of screen time in exchange for completing their tasks. For kids, they sign in to the mobile or web app and see their assigned chores for the day. They can also see possible rewards and learn how many chores they need to do to redeem them. This app has a long history of success with parents. As *The New York Times* says in its review of ChoreMonster, "It may sound like a lot of work to set up, but it was very easy, and in my tests worked reliably."

Teens: Craft a screen time and media contract

For your teens at home, when you give them a smartphone, make it very clear that they have to sign a contract that outlines your family's screen time and media rules. Too many parents give technology to their kids and forget to remind them that they're the ones paying for the monthly bill, so their rules apply. Fortunately, there are plenty of places to go online to get such a media agreement template. The Family Online Safety Institute (**fosi.org**) is probably one of the best sites to sift through some sample documents. Their downloadable "Family Online Safety Contract" includes a 12-step agreement outlining proper usage. It's easy enough to simply copy and paste this information, and then add your own custom rules about screen time. As *WebMD* suggests on their site, here are a couple more things you can add to your teen's screen time and media contract: no screen time during meals (at home or at restaurants) and no phone time until after homework is done.

Now that you're armed with some general best practices, here are a few helpful apps that can make managing screen time at home a bit easier. Most importantly, this puts you–the parent–back in control.

Screen Time Management Apps

Screentime (**www.screentimelabs.com**)

One of the things that we like about this app is that it is developed by another parent, a father of three boys, so he has a great sense of what works and what doesn't. This download works similarly to giving your child an allowance in that you essentially exchange the idea of money for screen time. In other words, you can assign daily, weekly, or custom screen time minutes. If your child chooses to give up screen time for other rewards, that is also an option (but don't hold your breath on this one!). Remember, this is not a monitoring app, but instead an app to assign screen time to your kids. Similar to what we mentioned above with ChoreMonster, you can also give extra screen time in exchange for chores. At the top of each child's profile, you will see the available screen time they have as per your assigned schedule and the time they have left that is unused or banked.

Kidslox (**www.kidslox.com**)

This is a beautifully designed cross-platform service that enables parents to set screen time boundaries. Aside from managing schedules, it will also let you block access to certain apps. If you download the iPhone version, for example, you can add a list of devices that you want to monitor (phones and tablets). When you enable Kidslox mode on a device, you can then choose restrictions. For instance, you can block the phone's browser so surfing the web is not allowed, but you can allow certain apps to work. Most importantly, in context of screen time, you can create a custom schedule for each child. You can enable Internet access on a device for a 30-minute window after dinner. This makes it a cinch to block access during important times, such as meal time, homework time, and bedtime. It's as simple as one tap to move a device from normal mode to restricted mode. Furthermore, you can also enable a technology time out so that the lock screen inhibits all access.

DinnerTime Plus (**www.dinnertimeapp.com**)

If you are tired of your kids on their phones and tablets at the dinner table, this app can help. While each version has different functionality (based on the specific platform), the goal again here is to allow parents to remind children about the importance of no screens at meal time, homework time, and bedtime. Through the parent app, you can set time limits, monitor real-time usage, block apps, and view reports. The app needs to be installed on both the parent's device and the child's device (you can add a second phone so both Mom and Dad have access). While the app is free, there is a one-time unlocking charge to get access to reports and to increase the number of devices you manage from two to five. Depending on whether you're managing iPhones or Android devices, the app operates in different ways due to the manufacturer's policies.

Computer Security

Your child's computer contains an enormous amount of personal and valuable information. He or she probably accesses multiple computers every day, including desktops and laptops at home or school. These devices store passwords, documents, photos, videos, email, and other digital communication. The security of your child's computer is the first step to securing all of your family's online devices and data. Predators and hackers will often target the weakest link in your home's digital configuration. Entire books have been written about computer security; however, we will focus only on the vital responsibilities. The majority of this section will focus on software-based solutions for Microsoft Windows operating systems. The end of the section will discuss Macintosh systems and physical vulnerabilities with any computer. We highly recommend that you read this entire chapter before attempting any of the following techniques. All security software recommendations are 100 percent free of cost and have no trial period limitations.

Microsoft Windows

Most readers of this book will possess computers that use a version of Microsoft Windows for an operating system. The most common versions include Windows 10 and Windows 7. We will not be discussing Windows XP. If you are still using this operating system, please upgrade immediately. Microsoft is no longer supporting the software and many vulnerabilities in it will never be patched. We will also not be discussing Windows Vista and Windows 8. These operating systems represent a small number of users and are commonly undesired. The majority of the instruction for Windows 7 applies to Vista. The majority of instruction for Windows 10 applies to 8. While these cannot be interchanged for every tutorial, most should apply.

Securing the operating system is vital in protecting your family's computers from online threats. Thousands of hackers are constantly scanning Internet Protocol (IP) addresses looking for vulnerable computers that do not possess specific security patches. No matter which version of Windows you use, even if the computer is brand new, you should apply security patches weekly. Most versions of Windows will conduct this patching automatically if you allow it. The following instructions will demonstrate how to make sure that your computer system is automatically updated when a new security patch is released. Your computer must be connected to the Internet to download any updates.

Windows 7

Click on the "Start" button on the lower left portion of the screen. In the right column, click "Control Panel." Click the last option, "Windows Update." Click on "Change Settings" and review the options. For optimum results, make sure that all boxes are checked.

Click "OK" to close this window. If you made any changes, you may want to click "Check for Updates" to manually download any pending security updates for your system. If this automatic setting was disabled for some time, or you are setting up a new computer, it may take up to an hour to retrieve and install all of the updates. Many updates will require you to reboot your system. After reboot, you should check for new updates. After you have your system completely updated, you will probably only notice updates once a week. Your computer will conduct the updates automatically and finish the process upon restarting.

Windows 10

Open Windows Update by swiping in from the right edge of the screen (or, if you're using a mouse, pointing to the lower-right corner of the screen and moving the mouse pointer up), tapping or clicking "Settings," tapping or clicking "Change PC settings," and then tapping or clicking "Update and recovery." Next, tap or click "Choose how updates get installed." Under "Important updates," choose the option that you want. Under "Recommended updates," select the "Give me recommended updates the same way I receive important updates" checkbox. Under "Microsoft Update," select the "Give me updates for other Microsoft products when I update Windows" checkbox, and then tap or click "Apply."

This brings up a common question that we receive during our presentations. Many people ask whether they should turn their computer off at night or just leave it on all of the time. There are many different opinions on this, but we firmly believe that you should turn your computer off at night, or when it will not be used for an extended period of time. The reasons are listed below.

- Specific hardware in the computer, including the standard hard drive, has a limited life. Since it has moving parts, every standard hard drive will fail eventually. The less time that your computer is on, the less time the hard drive is spinning at 7200 revolutions per minute (RPM).

- When a computer is turned off, it cannot respond to digital attacks. Many hacking attempts occur at night when systems are not in use.

- Turning off your wireless router and Internet connection device when not in use will provide even more protection.

- Turning the computer off when not in use will save energy.

Now that you have your Windows operating system updated and are receiving new security patches, you need to enable other software that will monitor your system for malicious software. We recommend the default option of Windows Defender.

Windows Defender

If you are using Windows 7 or newer, you have an option called Windows Defender in your control panel. This is probably already turned on and this icon will open the settings. Unless the service is turned off, you need to do nothing. However, if the service is indeed off, follow the on-screen instructions to activate the program. This program will continuously monitor the files on your computer and eliminate any malicious files that it identifies. While this is a great layer of protection against some malware, it is not a complete solution and provides no protection against computer viruses. For this, you will need a reliable antivirus program.

Antivirus

There are dozens of popular antivirus solutions for Windows-based systems. Many are not free and can cost more than $100 annually. Only free solutions will be discussed in this book. Antivirus programs run continuously and monitor all activity. This includes any time you open a document, launch a program, or download a file from the Internet. The program scans all new files and quarantines any files that are suspicious. It will usually then prompt you for action. There are two very important things to consider when configuring your antivirus program.

The first is to make sure that your program is receiving updates. We have seen computers that possess an expired version of premium software that is no longer receiving any updates. This is the same as having no antivirus software at all. The second important detail is to make sure you only have one antivirus program installed on the computer. This is a situation where more is actually less. If you have more than one antivirus program, they will battle each other for authority over your system. If you have an expired premium software package, such as Norton or McAfee, and you do not plan on renewing the service, you should uninstall it completely. If you currently have a paid or free version of premium software, and you have verified that it is functioning and receiving updates, you should leave it on the computer and disregard installation steps for the next program, Microsoft Security Essentials. However, if you believe, as we do, that some of these premium software packages slow your computer down, you may want to consider replacing your current program.

Windows 7

If you want to stick with security programs created by Microsoft, Security Essentials is your only option. This free program is provided and maintained by Microsoft and will work on any version of Windows from XP through 7. This software is not included with any of these versions of Windows and must be downloaded and installed. The following steps will complete the installation.

- Navigate to the website:
  windows.microsoft.com/en-us/windows/security-essentials-download.

- Click on the "Get it now" button.

- Execute the downloaded file and allow the default choices.

If successful, you should see a green window when launching the program from either your start menu or the status bar in the lower right portion of your screen.

Windows 10

Many new computers now arrive with Windows 10 installed. This new operating system is very different than every other version of Windows. Antivirus software is already installed on Windows 10. This software is also called Windows Defender, but should not be confused with previous versions of Windows Defender for older operating systems. The new software replaces Security Essentials and is free for all users of Windows 10. If your new computer came pre-configured with a trial edition of antivirus software, such as Norton or McAfee, you will need to uninstall the trial software before you enable Windows Defender. Personally, we recommend the free Windows Defender program for Windows 10 computers.

UAC

Windows 7 and 10 users have a default security option called User Access Control (UAC). This security setting mandates that your operating system prompt you for approval when any unauthorized program wants to make changes to your operating system. The display will include darkening your screen and presenting you with a box asking if you approve the action. This is a huge layer of security, especially with malicious websites. Some websites will try to load and execute malicious software on your computer without your permission. When this happens, UAC prevents the action unless you approve it. Overall, if you are ever presented with the UAC prompt, and you did nothing to warrant the action, decline permission by clicking "No." Some legitimate programs will activate this dialogue when you execute the program. When this happens, allowing the action is fine, as you are the one who initiated the program launch.

This step is vital for computers used by children. Kids often click without thinking and like to visit questionable websites. They do not know the ramifications of visiting illegal music download sites or file sharing services offering free movies. These are riddled with viruses. We encourage you to explain to your children that the screen going dark and asking for approval is almost always a bad sign. Saying "yes" to these requests will likely bring in malicious software and immediate infection to your computer system.

Hopefully you now have a computer system that will receive all security and program updates; is blocking incoming malicious software; has antivirus software configured; and will prompt you if bad programs try to make changes. You are now ready to install supplemental malicious software detection.

Malicious Software Removal

At this point, you are probably asking yourself why you would need more additional protection than the products already discussed. You may also feel that adding more protection is too difficult and you may want to abandon installing more programs. Unfortunately, there is no one program that will catch and remove all malicious software. In fact, if you encounter a program that makes this claim, it is probably a virus in disguise. We would avoid any product that guarantees to stop all intrusions. If you have successfully downloaded the programs that were previously discussed, they are now monitoring your system and you need to take no additional action. The following programs in this section do not necessarily monitor your system at all times. They are present on your system and waiting to be executed. After the programs are explained, we will recommend a schedule for executing each package.

CCleaner (Windows)

CCleaner is one of our favorite programs ever created. It provides a simple interface and is used to clean potentially unwanted files and invalid Windows Registry entries from your computer. This software works on both Windows and Mac computers. The following steps will download and install the free version of the application.

- Navigate to **www.piriform.com/ccleaner/download**

- In the "Free" column, click on "download." You will see this under a heading titled "Download from." This will ensure that you download the free version.

- Execute the program and accept the default installation settings.

After the installation completes, launch the program. You have several options under the Cleaner tab that will allow you to choose the data to eliminate. The default options are the safest. Clicking on the "Analyze" button will allow the program to identify files to delete without committing to the removal. This will allow you to view the files before clicking "Run Cleaner" to remove them. If you are running this program on a computer with heavy Internet usage, you may be surprised at the amount of unnecessary files present. The first time you use this program, the removal process can take several minutes or possibly an hour. If you run the program monthly, it will finish the process much quicker.

The Registry tab of CCleaner will eliminate unnecessary and missing registry entries. This can help your computer operate more efficiently. The default options on this menu are most appropriate. Click on "Scan For Issues" and allow it to identify any problems. This process should go quickly. When complete, click on "Fix Selected Issues" to complete the process.

The Tools tab provides an easy way to disable specific programs from launching when your computer starts. These programs can slow your computer down when they are running unnecessarily. These can be found by clicking the "Startup" button in the left column. Selecting the "Disable" button marks programs and prevents them from launching the next time the computer starts. If you want to reverse this, you can select the entries again and choose "Enable."

After cleaning out any temporary and unnecessary files, we recommend the first scan for malicious files on your computer. There are dozens of options for this, but we believe Malware Bytes is the best. The following instructions will provide the desired protection.

- Navigate to **www.malwarebytes.org** and select the "Download" option.

- This will forward you to a second page to choose the version. Select "Download Free."

- Execute the file and accept the default installation options.

After you have installed the application, you must execute it in order to run a scan. Malware Bytes does not run in the background as an antivirus program does. We recommend that you perform a scan at least once monthly. The following steps should be taken every time you run the program.

- Click on the "Update" tab and choose "Check for Updates."

- If any updates are available, allow the program to install the updates.

- Under the "Scanner" tab, choose the default option of "Perform full scan" and click "Scan." Choose the drives you want to scan. We recommend that you check the C drive and any other hard drives attached to your computer. The program will automatically scan your computer and remove any threats. You will receive a report at the end.

Schedule

We will confess to being more cautious than the average computer user. Years of investigating computer crime and technology will do that to you. Personally, we scan our Windows computers every week for any signs of malicious software. That may be overkill for you. Our recommendation to the general audience is that you should be conducting a complete scan of your computer at least once per month. This includes launching, updating, and executing CCleaner and Malware Bytes. After that, you should scan your computer with your antivirus, even though it is always running. Performing this monthly task will keep you protected from the most common threats. It will also provide a more secure environment for your child's random browsing.

Macintosh

One common question that we often receive is "Are Mac products safer than Windows?" This is not a clear yes or no answer. First, we should state that there absolutely are several viruses and malicious programs designed for the Mac. That being said, the amount is nothing near those that are designed for Windows computers. It is estimated that more than 48 million new unique malware exploits were found in 2015. More than 98 percent were written for the Windows operating system. Less than 5,000 new viruses were written for Mac OS X.

Overall, it will depend on your family's activity. If you are checking email and visiting popular websites, you are very unlikely to get a virus on a Mac. Visiting those same websites will put you in danger if you are on a Windows machine. For the purposes of full disclosure, we strictly use MacBook Pro laptops for all of our computer needs. We would never consider operating in Windows without good antivirus and malware protection, and we rarely conduct a virus scan on our Macs. If your family uses Mac computers during heavy amounts of Internet browsing, we have two recommendations.

CCleaner (Mac)

As mentioned earlier, CCleaner is one of our favorite applications for a Windows computer. The Mac version does not have as many options as the Windows version. However, we still run a scan monthly to delete temporary files and other cached data. The program looks very similar to the Windows version, and operates in the same manner as described earlier. CCleaner can be found through the Mac App Store or by searching "CCleaner Mac" in any search engine.

Sophos (Mac)

There is always much debate within Mac user groups about the necessity of antivirus software on a Mac. One camp believes that you must have the latest virus definitions and allow a real-time scan to run continuously to catch threats. The other camp believes that you do not need an antivirus solution and that you can download one later if you somehow receive a virus. We sit in the middle of these two beliefs. We think that every family Mac computer should have antivirus software installed, updated, and ready to go. Here are the instructions for setting up this type of maintenance.

- Navigate to **www.sophos.com/en-us/products/free-tools/sophos-antivirus-for-mac-home-edition-legacy.aspx**

- The "Get Started" button on this page will download the software to your computer after supplying any name to their contact fields. You can also search through the Mac App Store for this same software.

- Install the program either through the App Store or by double clicking the downloaded file and following the default instructions.

- Click on the new shield icon in the menu bar and select "Update Now." Allow the updater to collect any new virus definitions. This may take several minutes.

- To run a monthly scan, click on the shield logo and select "Scan Local Drives." This will scan any hard drives or flash drives connected for any known vulnerabilities.

Passwords

Regardless of the operating system that your family uses, secure passwords are mandatory in order to protect your child's online accounts. The most common attack from an online bully is through a weak password. Children usually choose very simple and short passwords. When malicious schoolmates learn of this vulnerability, they use it to exploit a child. Bullies might use this access to read your child's personal messages. Once in the account, an imposter could post harmful messages from your child's account, causing further turmoil. While this commonly applies to email and social network profiles, strong password policies should be enabled on all sensitive accounts. While we could write an entire book about password cracking and sniffing, brute-force and dictionary attacks, and overall complexity, we will instead focus on the most vital pieces that every parent should know. The following password security protocols should be implemented on every online account that possesses sensitive information. This also includes your own accounts! At the end, we will simplify our approach.

Password Complexity: We have all been lectured many times about creating strong passwords. This is to prevent automated computer attacks that try common words and then add a number or two at the end. Fast computers can make thousands of attempts per second. Strong passwords prevent this type of attack because the complexity would require millions of guesses that would take many months or years to crack. The following guidelines apply to any sensitive accounts.

- Passwords should have at least ten characters.
- At least one character should be uppercase.

- Passwords should have at least one special character ($, &, %).
- Passwords should have at least two numbers.

Password Variety: Many of us recycle our passwords within multiple websites. We have adopted a secure credential that we like and use it everywhere. This is extremely risky behavior. If a hacker steals your child's Twitter password, he or she would also have the password for an email account. Most children use the same password for everything. When one account gets hacked, they all become compromised. Possessing a unique password for each account prevents this type of attack.

Password Auto-Save: Your child's web browser offers to save all passwords for easy entry when a site is visited. While this is very convenient, it exposes a large attack surface. If a friend of your child uses his or her computer to visit Facebook, it will automatically populate your child's user name and password. This can be too much temptation for a nosy friend. Additionally, computer viruses are known to share this stored data with the hackers who create them.

Password Updates: At an extreme minimum, your child's sensitive passwords should be changed yearly. If there is suspicion that an account has been accessed without authorization, you should increase the frequency of updates.

Password Storage: We mentioned previously that we do not encourage children to save their passwords within web browsers. Our solution might be quite surprising. We encourage parents to have their children write them on paper. Parents can then keep a copy to provide when the child loses his or her own copy. While this technique may seem outdated, there is no computer hacker in the world who can steal this piece of paper through the Internet.

Security Questions: While not directly related to passwords, parents must also be concerned with the security questions associated with their child's accounts. Most email and social network services require a child to select one or more security questions when an account is created. The child must also supply the answers to these questions. If the child is ever locked out of an account, a security question can be answered for immediate access. Unfortunately, children often choose poor security questions such as "What is your favorite color?" or "What is your school mascot?" We encourage parents to teach their children to execute one of the following two options.

- Choose security questions with answers that are difficult to guess.
- Provide false answers to commonly known security questions.

Many parents might be thinking that their children will never comply with all of this. These tips can seem intimidating at first, but we believe that they can be simplified. Assume that your child likes the password of "rabbit," and he or she is not willing to budge. This word alone is not secure, but adding digits to it can make it acceptable. His or her password list might appear as follows.

Email: Rabbit@2016@
Facebook: Rabbit!2016!
Twitter: Rabbit#2016#
Instagram: Rabbit^2016^

Each of these passwords seem very similar. The only content that is different is the special character used within each. The "@" might remind the child of an email address; the "!" could relate to the excitement on Facebook; the "#" represents a hashtag on Twitter; and the "^" could be associated with "uploading" photos to Instagram. It is important that the child picks the special character for each service. More importantly, we have met the criteria for each of the previous tips. When 2017 arrives, it can be an indicator of an expired password that should be updated. These options are not foolproof. A savvy bully could learn this method after stealing a couple of passwords; however, this is unlikely. Applying these principles will make your child more secure than most everyone else in his or her circles.

Mobile Device Security

Today's smartphones are computers. Every Android, iPhone, Windows phone, and Blackberry possesses a processor, RAM, and an operating system. Your child's current cellular telephone has more computer power than our first four PCs combined; therefore, you should secure them as well as a traditional computer, if not better. As your children rely on these portable devices for their daily communication, it is possible there is more personal information stored on the telephone than any other computer device you own. It is likely that all of their email communication, text messages, contacts, appointments, and documents are available through their telephones. More importantly, their various user names and passwords are probably stored for easy access. Fortunately, this can all be protected by being aware of the threats targeting portable devices.

Passcodes

When it comes to smartphone safety, the single most important thing a mobile telephone owner can do is lock the device with a passcode. The passcode will need to be entered before a user can access any data or functions of the device. This may be a unique PIN, a password, a specific swipe, or a pattern drawn with your finger connecting a series of dots. Every smartphone should have some type of lockout function enabled. This security will make the device useless if it is stolen and will protect any of your child's personal information. Each type of device will have a unique way of programming this feature. It will commonly be found under "Settings" and then "Screen lock." Some newer devices will completely erase the content if the wrong code is entered ten times.

The most secure option is either a password or a PIN longer than four digits. A four-digit number is fairly easy to crack and the number of users with a PIN of "1234" is shocking. A swipe pattern can be secure only if it is complicated. If a device has a pattern screen lock that is preventing a malicious friend or bully from accessing the data, he or she needs to know the proper swipe sequence to get into the phone. Holding the telephone at an angle may allow them to see a defined smudge mark that appears to make a pattern around the perimeter of the screen. Replicating this pattern might grant full access to the device. Criminals use this technique to break into a victim's stolen telephone.

Device Tracking

Many people have heard about cellular tracking software, but few apply it. These are the programs or settings that you configure on your child's telephone, and they reside quietly until needed. If the device is lost or stolen, you can remotely enable the application through a web browser and the response will display the GPS coordinates of the telephone's current location. Both Android and iPhone offer this as a free service, but most people only consider tracking software when it is too late. It is usually only after a phone is stolen that the idea of tracking software is considered.

Fortunately, technology has advanced and we can sometimes apply tracking solutions even after a device is missing.

Android

Android Device Manager is Google's official and easy-to-use tool to track your Android phone or tablet. The best thing about it is that you don't need to install an app to be able to track your child's devices. The only requirement is that the device is connected to your Google account, turned on, and connected to the Internet. All you need to do is visit the Android Device Manager while being logged into your Google Account. Once the site is loaded, it will automatically try to track down your phone. If you have several Android devices registered, make sure the right one is chosen in the dropdown menu.

In a recent update, Google implemented some features into their search results page. This means that you're able to quickly locate any registered Android device right from the search results. By using the search phrase "where is my phone," Google displays a small map above the search results in which it will try to find your phone. Once found, you can let it ring by clicking on "Ring" at the bottom left. While a bit creepy, it should work when you need it.

iPhone

The latest iPhones have this tracking capability built into the device. However, you do need to activate the service from the telephone before it can be tracked. To enable the location feature, go to "Settings" and select "iCloud." Toggle the option for "Find My iPhone" to "ON." Your child's telephone is now capable of being tracked through your iCloud account. To track the current location of the telephone, conduct the following tasks.

- Log into your iCloud account through **icloud.com** from any computer.

- Click on "Devices" in the upper-left corner and select the device you want to locate.

If the device is online, its approximate location is shown on the map. This may take a few minutes. The green circle around the device indicates the area where the device is located. The smaller the circle, the better the accuracy. If "Find My iPhone" cannot locate this device, the last known location is displayed for up to 24 hours, after which the map is cleared. You can select the "Notify Me When Found" checkbox to receive an email when the device comes back online with a location.

Exif Data

Cellular telephones have become the primary digital camera for most users. Every digital photograph captured with a cellular telephone camera possesses metadata known as EXIF data. This is a layer of code that provides information about the photo and camera. All digital cameras write this data to each image, but the amount and type of data can vary. This data is embedded into each photo "behind the scenes" and is not visible by viewing the captured image. You need an EXIF reader, which can be found on websites and within applications. The easiest way to see the information is through an online viewer such as Jeffrey's EXIF Viewer at **regex.info//exif.cgi**.

The main security concern with this data is the presence of GPS information within the photograph. All current cellular telephone cameras now include GPS identification as an option. If the GPS is turned on, and your child did not disable geotagging of the photos in the camera settings, the device will store location data within the EXIF data of the photo. Figure 7.01 displays the analysis of an image taken with a camera with GPS. The location field translated the captured GPS coordinates from the photo and identified the location where the photo was captured. Figure 7.02 displays a satellite view map from a photo taken in Florida on an Android cellular telephone. All Android and iPhone devices have this capability. Your default settings will vary by device.

This technology exposes your child to risk. When he or she uploads digital photos to the Internet, the action may be revealing the home or school of the child. Child predators look for this information when monitoring a potential victim. Stalkers use this information to identify new locations of their victims.

What does this mean for your child? When he or she captures and posts photos to social networks or photo-sharing websites, the activity may be announcing the location of every step that is taken. While this may not seem a harsh threat to adults, consider your child who constantly uploads photos from the phone. Can his or her home, school, and friends' houses be easily identified from this data? Our recommendation is to disable this feature. The instructions for all four major device operating systems are listed here.

- Android: Enter the Camera feature of the device. Click on the "Settings" menu, choose "GPS tag" or "Location," and select "Off."

- iPhone: Launch Settings and select "Location Services." Toggle the Camera option to "Off."

- Blackberry: Enter the Camera feature of the device. Select the Location icon and set it to "Disabled."

- Windows Phone: Launch Settings and navigate to the Applications option. Open the Pictures and Camera tab and set the GPS option to "Off."

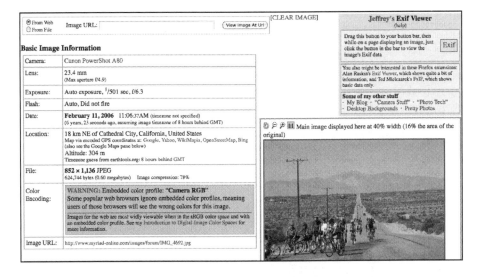

Figure 7.01: A Jeffrey's EXIF Viewer result identifying location.

Figure 7.02: A Jeffrey's EXIF Viewer result displaying a satellite view of location data.

Summary

We've now reviewed many of the key strategies parents need to follow in terms of managing screen time. As we mentioned above, screen time risks include a number of things: sleep disturbances, social disturbances, eye health disturbances, and other possible health issues, such as obesity. While we may not notice monthly changes in terms of time online, there are a number of reports that show the shocking increase in how much time new generations of kids are spending in front of screens.

In a 2015 *BBC* article on this topic, *Childwise's* "The Connected Kids" report outlines how UK children, ages five to sixteen, consume content. The organization has been consistently collecting data over the course of twenty years (starting in 1995). What they've discovered over this period is that children are now spending more than twice the time in front of a screen than they were spending just two decades ago (three hours then compared to six and a half hours today in front of some type of electronic device). At the top of this screen time list are teen boys, a group that easily spends up to eight hours a day in front of a screen. On the bottom of this list are eight-year-old girls who spend about three and half hours in front of a screen.

The study cites that one of the biggest differences today compared to 1995 is that we, both adults and kids, are engaging in multi-screen viewing. It's easy to see how this is true in many homes, yours included. Take a moment to count the number of different devices your family owns. For example, kids today now have access to televisions, gaming consoles, tablets, smartphones, and other screen-based products.

In the US alone, according to *Yahoo! Tech*, the average house has five to ten connected devices. As we detail in Chapter 11, the rise of the Internet of Things means that the number of these everyday tech gadgets will skyrocket very quickly to include wearables (such as smart watches), appliances (such as smart fridges), and virtual reality headsets (such as Samsung Gear VR). In fact, the Organization for Economic Co-operation and Development says that by 2022 the average family, with two kids in their teens, will own about 50 Internet-connected devices.

As the *BBC* states in their The Connected Kids article: "Ubiquitous online access is also likely to influence the way children interact with their families and their willingness to participate in family holidays and trips out." With kids spending so many of their waking hours in front of screens, and with so many slick new connected products coming to the market, it's especially important today for parents to step up screen time monitoring efforts. This should include a combination of monitoring the content they're consuming and the actual time they're spending consuming it (and now you have a few great apps to do the latter).

In the next chapter, we will expand on some of the more serious risks associated with screen time online. This will include targeted attacks from bullies, predators, and hackers. We will explain common avenues that these groups use to get access to your preschoolers, preteens, and teens. Since we've reviewed in detail many of the social media risks, next we will also talk about the rise of bullying online and what you can to do as a parent to end this problem.

A Question from a Parent

Brian Segulich: I would like to know how to talk to our kids about why we're doing all of this and how to gradually educate them on the dangers. I'm hoping that some best practice approaches can be shared, as well as learning what could be done differently next time.

Amber's Answer: We outline screen time best practices and apps within this section. Another thing we want to reinforce is to keep an open dialogue with your child. While some of their actions online may upset you, the last thing you want is for them to shut down on you. If, while reading this book, you can pick up and try some of the services your kids are using, you will have a much better chance of talking to them about some of the issues they're encountering in a language they understand. You will also be in a better position when it comes to screen time to recommend premium content and activities; in the case of all kids, this means exploring the thousands of educational sites and apps that exist today. While you might think you will get some eye rolls from your kids on this front, if you show them something interesting online you can share together, you just might be surprised to find out they respect your willingness to learn. Too many parents give up when it comes to managing screen time, but it's a battle worth fighting as early on in your child's online life as possible. A young child without boundaries is going to run into potential problems later in life on the Internet.

Chapter Eight
Targeted Attacks

Throughout this chapter we will talk about three types of targeted attacks, which include bullies, predators, and hackers. Many children will experience some form of online bullying in their lives, whether they are bullying (which no parent likes to believe) or they're being bullied. We'll also talk about different ways that predators approach your children online. When your kids hit their teen years, these attacks get much more dangerous and can often involve some form of blackmail. With hackers, while we're all at risk, we'll talk specifically about how these groups use phishing scams to target young people who are avid social media users (which, if you have teen children, probably describes them to a tee).

When it comes to defining the number of kids bullied, we've seen reports that indicate that half of all children are victims of some type of bullying (and a lot of this behavior starts and continues online). Even worse, according to the i-SAFE foundation, more than one in three young people have experienced cyber threats online. This same organization also reported another disturbing fact: more than half of young people do not tell their parents when bullying does occur. We could go on for this entire chapter citing different studies and surveys about online bullying and where we're at today with this unfortunate trend. In severe cases, this abuse can lead to suicide, which is why we're seeing a rise in the number of organizations that are launching to help kids deal with these new digital pressures.

If we're trying to figure out the number of children who are victims of predators, similar to finding updated recommendations for screen time, many organizations share outdated stats that reflect the Internet landscape five or ten years ago. For example, a leading Canadian child safety media organization includes public stats from between the years of 2002 and 2007. Today, with the increase in how much kids are present online, and the prevalence of social media networking and messaging services, their chances of encountering a predator are much more likely than we're probably comfortable admitting.

As we described during the Screen Time chapter, this likelihood is due to the reality that our kids have access to more connected devices than ever before and there is an evolving perception about the definition of a "friend."

PureSight.com reinforces this behavior (while most of the stats below are more than 5 years old, the general message about how kids are behaving online applies).

- Teens are willing to meet with strangers: 16 percent of teens considered meeting someone they've only talked to online and 8 percent have actually met someone they only knew online.

- 75 percent of children are willing to share personal information online about themselves and their family in exchange for goods and services.

- 33 percent of teens are Facebook friends with people they have not met face to face.

The one bit of information we do have that is up-to-date, which is good news for hackers and bad news for digital citizens, is how careless we all are with our passwords. For the fifth year in a row, according to *SplashData* (2015), the most popular password in America and in Western Europe is "123456." Yes, we can do better, and we owe it to our kids to teach them how to effectively choose passwords that will protect their privacy and security.

Since your child is probably dealing with online bullies, or knows someone who is, let's start there with some common attacks and strategies on how to deal with them.

Online Bullying

We should first make the distinction between in-person bullying and online bullying. While they are both hurtful, there are important differences. When we mention online bullying, we essentially mean the same thing as cyberbullying. In a 2015 New Zealand publication "Bullying Prevention and Response" study, they define cyberbullying as follows:

"Cyberbullying is one particular form of bullying. It is bullying that is enabled, enhanced, or in some way mediated through digital technology. Digital technology can be a medium for all kinds of bullying behavior, including physical, verbal and social / relational bullying. Cyberbullying is becoming more prevalent and involves using email, cellular phones, chat rooms, social networking sites and instant messaging to bully others verbally, socially or psychologically."

Bullying is not just a Canadian or an American problem. In fact, events such as The International Day of Pink reach worldwide audiences that are actively working together to end bullying in schools and communities. This particular campaign started in 2007 and now millions of people participate every year.

This movement started after two grade 12 boys stood up to defend a grade 9 student who was bullied for wearing pink to school. That night, the older boys at Central Kings Rural High School in Nova Scotia bought 50 pink shirts at a local discount store and went online to ask classmates to wear the shirts the next day. Not only did the kids wear these new shirts, many more showed up in their own pink clothing to defend the boy. Here is how one of the older boys, who organized the campaign, described to *CBC.ca* the moment the younger bullied boy walked into school to a sea of pink:

"Definitely it looked like there was a big weight lifted off his shoulders. He went from looking right depressed to being as happy as can be. If you can get more people against them... to show that we're not going to put up with it and support each other, then they're not as big as a group as they think they are."

While some bullying does start in person, it very often continues online and becomes even more frequent and severe. Technology makes it too easy for a bully to harass. For starters, bullies can post anonymously on many different websites, never forced to be face to face with the person they're bullying. Also, these hurtful messages spread more easily, quickly circulating to large groups of people thanks to the prevalence of social media (just think how easy it is to forward a text or re-share a post). This means that online bullying can involve massive groups of people; can occur at any time of the day; and can leave a permanent record in the digital playground (it's also easier to get away with online bullying than face-to-face bullying). All of these things can wreak havoc on your child if they are a victim.

In the next section, we will address the types of online bullying, where bullying happens the most online (social media and gaming), and what parents, teachers, and kids can do about it.

Harassment

In this instance, the bully frequently sends and/or posts offensive messages to a person. In other words, this isn't simply a one-off activity. For a teen, this could include a bully sending daily unsolicited or threatening messages. It can also include a constant stream of defamatory comments on a teen's social media accounts. Also, harassment is common during live text chats or video streaming. With the rise of services such as Periscope and Facebook Live, we'll likely see a lot more of this in the next few years. Like all online bullying cases, it's important to keep accurate records of any harassing activity.

Flaming

When we describe these different types of online bullying, you will notice that there is a lot of overlap in terms of the bully's behavior. In the case of flaming, this is written, verbal, or emotional abuse. The person doing the flaming, the flamer, will purposefully write things to torment his or her victim. In most cases, they are looking for a reaction, which is why it's good advice for the person being flamed to simply ignore this behavior. It's also very possible that the person who is subject to flaming has no idea at first that this is happening, as the bully will gradually pull that person into a seemingly innocent conversation and then impulsively attack.

Exclusion

Many children online are simply seeking inclusion, wanting to be part of a community or group. That is why this form of bullying often hurts the most. Exclusion is when a person or group of people decide to leave another individual out of a conversation or chat. In effect, they gang up on that particular person. When they target this particular child, they then decide to reject them from any of their group's online activities.

Outing

All of the above are devastating to children, and outing is another example of a form of online bullying that can negatively affect a child's overall well-being. While some kids assume that chatting when using ephemeral messaging services such as Snapchat (disappearing social media) is private without any type of permanent record, it's quite common for a recipient to screenshot a private note or image and then share it with other people to out the sender. Many times, if a child sends a personal message that is sexual in nature (or just plain embarrassing), the recipient will share with other people as a form of outing.

Masquerading

This is a more elaborate form of bullying, and unfortunately, it occurs quite often. This is when a bully goes to great lengths to pretend to be someone else. They will create an email address using a peer's name, launch a social media account using a peer's photo, or sign up for a messaging app with a peer's info. This is a common occurrence on social media sites. While the bully pretends to be another child online, they will share messages and images that are embarrassing and hurtful. Throughout this entire time, the bully's identity is hidden.

Cyberstalking

This is an extreme form of harassment. These non-stop messages and comments are often threatening. In a lot of these cases, the individual who is cyberstalked is fearful that the bully will show up at their house or school in person. This is why, as we explained earlier in the book, that children need to be especially careful about protecting their personal information online, such as their location and their school. If this content gets into the hands of someone who is cyberstalking them, an already horrible situation can escalate quickly.

Bullying in Social Media

Throughout the book, we touch on cases of bullying in social media. Whether your child is using Twitter, Instagram, Facebook, or other social apps, there are always bullies nearby who are skilled enough to prey on them (sometimes they might even be their best friends). Online bullying tactics include all of the above, but what's most worrisome is that some parents don't look upon these situations seriously enough.

Again, one of the problems is that we just don't have recent statistics to show how detrimental online bullying can be in today's world. What we do know is that, for victims, in-person bullying can be a factor that leads to horrible outcomes including suicide. In all cases, both the bully and the person being bullied are more likely to experience depression.

In 17-year-old Rehtaeh Parson's case, extreme bullying led to suicide. The Nova Scotia teen alleged that a group of boys gang raped her when she was just 15 years old. After one of the boys took a photo during their sexual encounter, he shared it with a couple of friends. The image quickly made the rounds to kids at her school and beyond. After more than a year of harassment (in this case, mostly slut shaming, a common bullying tactic), she attempted suicide by hanging. Rehtaeh was fighting for her life in a coma, but after four days with very little progress, her parents made the devastating decision on April 7, 2013 to switch off her life support.

As her mother told CNN in 2013, "Rehtaeh is gone today because of the four boys that thought that raping a 15-year-old girl was OK and to distribute a photo to ruin her spirit and reputation would be fun. All the bullying and messaging and harassment that never let up are also to blame. Lastly, the justice system failed her. Those are the people that took the life of my beautiful girl."

The story made headlines around the world. In fact, it's still making headlines. In the fall of 2014, two boys pled guilty; the first to making child pornography and the second to distributing child pornography. Rehtaeh's suicide inspired a cyberbullying law in Nova Scotia, which became central to another case, but resulted in the act being struck down by the Nova Scotia Supreme Court in 2015. However, the Canadian province is drafting new legislation. As Nova Scotia Attorney General and Justice Minister Diana Whalen said in media releases discussing this legislation:

"We feel strongly there is a need for us to recognize the changing world of technology and the world our young people are part of. We want to protect them," she said in an interview with *The Globe and Mail*. "There was a gap, and remains a gap for the whole country. We definitely recognize it here in the wake of a tragedy."

"The Department of Justice accepts the court's ruling that the definition of cyberbullying in the former act was overly broad and will not appeal the court's decision. Instead, a new act will be drafted that addresses the court's concerns and ensures Nova Scotians have a high level of protection when faced with cyberbullies."

Amanda Todd's story is equally as heartbreaking. The young British Columbia girl, born in 1996, met a stranger in a webcam chat room late in 2010 who convinced her to expose her breasts on camera. After doing so, a screen capture of her naked upper body made the rounds online. The man, who asked Amanda to flash him, tried to blackmail her, demanding that she put on a show for him or he would distribute the photo to her friends and family. He followed through on his threat, creating a Facebook profile with her topless image and sending it to various people at her school.

Amanda was severely bullied online, to the point where she changed schools a number of times. She was also physically assaulted. She attempted suicide after this attack, but was hospitalized and survived. However, the bullying continued for several months, and eventually Amanda was found dead, at age 15, after committing suicide at her home on October 12, 2012.

Although there were tips and red flags that things were going to end tragically, no one was able to do anything to save this young girl's life. In fact, just one month before her death, she shared a public video on YouTube called "My Story: Struggling, bullying, suicide and self-harm." Using flash cards while hiding her face, she described the attacks on tiny pieces of paper. Here is the last written statement she shared within the eight-minute video, which went viral after her death:

"Every day, I think, why am I still here? I'm stuck. What's left of me now? Nothing stops. I have nobody. I need someone. My name is Amanda Todd."

In April 2014, the Royal Canadian Mounted Police (RCMP) charged a 35-year-old man from the Netherlands with extortion, Internet luring, criminal harassment, and child pornography. Unsurprisingly, Amanda was not his only victim. *Nobullying.com* posted several media quotes from Amanda's mom, Carol Todd, following the girl's death:

"Technology has ramped it up so much that there are no boundaries. It's so faceless and they are free to say whatever, they're free to say and do whatever without thinking about it. The picture was put out there on the Internet and then all of a sudden, her peers started harassing her, both face-to-face bullying and online, so she had to endure that kind of abuse. She was afraid to go to school, people were looking at her, she developed more depression, social anxiety. She was afraid people were watching her all the time."

The following is from *BullyStatistics.org*:

"A recent study by the US National Institutes of Health, reported by Reuters, found that victims of cyberbullying showed more signs of depression than other bullying victims. This may be because cyberbullying can be more relentless and more frightening or discouraging, especially if the bully is anonymous."

Bullying in Gaming

While we've devoted many pages in this book to social media, we have not spent much time addressing another favorite pastime your child probably enjoys: gaming. If your child is playing online games with other participants, it's key to pay attention to those relationships. In fact, stats show that oftentimes bullying in gaming environments is higher than in other online activities, especially for girls. According to a *VentureBeat.com* story, 63 percent of female gamers have been sexually harassed in digital environments. They also describe different types of online bullying that are specific to video games to include the following.

Role-playing games: As gamers assume different personas, they often take on some of the character's more aggressive traits and end up bullying their opponents without that intention when they started.

Harassing messages: As gaming is competitive, participants often get aggressive and can send hurtful messages to their opponents that they would never say in real life.

Ganging up: As gamers work together, there are often cases when they work together to identify and then threaten a victim in the game.

Griefers: These gamers often look at harassing other gamers online as an enjoyable pastime or hobby, always on the prowl for victims.

Password theft & viruses: As gamers seem to be simply working to get to know their teammates or opponents, they may in fact be phishing for personal information to steal passwords or they may want to infect another gamer's computer with viruses.

While there are obvious online gaming risks, there are also many ways that gaming can help to educate our youngest digital citizens. We touched on the popularity of Minecraft earlier on in the book, but it's worth re-visiting to stress how simple virtual blocks lead kids into a world of possibilities. As *The New York Times* writes in its recent article on The Minecraft Generation:

"Nearly everyone who plays Minecraft, or even watches someone else do so, remarks on its feeling of freedom: All those blocks, infinities of them! Build anything you want! Players have recreated the Taj Mahal, the U.S.S. Enterprise from *Star Trek*, the entire capital city from Game of Thrones."

The article also talks about how the game encourages computational thinking, so kids are actively focused on solving problems and designing solutions. If you need to know more about how to build something, or if you need inspiration to build something, check out the more than 70 million instructional Minecraft videos on YouTube. In fact, according to Google, Minecraft is the second most searched term on the popular video-sharing site—the first is music.

Microsoft, which acquired Minecraft in 2014, is taking note of the game's potential on the learning front. Their new 2016 program, Minecraft: Education Edition, will provide teachers and students from more than 100 schools across 30 countries with the ability to test the beta program that will eventually be available on trial for free in 11 languages for educators.

The announcement included this note from Marie Lindsay, Principal of St. Mary's College in Northern Ireland:

"Minecraft takes learners on a journey where often, their answers are not yet known. We can join them, in their own context, and develop them as learners from where they are. Minecraft gives us as educators an opportunity to engage more fully, and I'm excited to embrace this so our young people will be better prepared for the world that awaits them."

What to Do About Bullying

In the next couple of chapters, we talk in depth about some helpful strategies in terms of reporting and online etiquette.

In terms of bullying, parents aren't the only group of people who are responsible for finding a solution. Parents, teachers, and kids must work together to fight online bullying, and to keep communities safe. For parents, we've reviewed many of the key steps to follow to ensure your kids are smart about user names and passwords. We've also discussed how apps can help you to monitor for potential issues. Plus, we've explained some common social media lingo. It's also important to explain to children that they need to talk to parents or teachers about online bullying; they will not do this if you overreact every time they take this approach.

Kids also have a responsibility to practice proper social media sharing, especially as they get into their teens. This means, as we've explained, no sharing passwords with friends. Also, they should understand that keeping a diary of what's happening if they are a victim of online bullying is a great way to manage the situation if things get worse. There are also ways that kids can help other kids who are bullied, either by defending them or talking to an adult if they are worried about that child's safety and well-being.

While teachers might feel as though their hands are tied when it comes to online bullying, they are absolutely part of the equation. They can work to ensure that their school's anti-bullying policies are up-to-date and include guidelines in reference to online bullying. They also have enormous power when it comes to educating children in the classroom and at assemblies about how to deal with bullies online.

Online Predators

In 1999, Michael conducted his first child solicitation sting while working as a police detective in the St. Louis, Missouri area. This was before the television show *To Catch A Predator* had been created, and there were still many unknowns in reference to proper computer crime investigation strategies. It was simply shocking to see the number of adult men trying to lure teenagers as young as 13 from an online Yahoo! chat room into a real-world meeting. They offered gifts, money, and favors in exchange for sex. The confidence of these criminals was staggering. The security of an anonymous chat room created an environment where rejection could be tolerated. Pedophiles who did not have the courage to approach a child in public could send dozens of messages a minute hoping for only one child to respond. It was a nightmare for the parents of children who became involved in these awful situations.

Numerous arrests were made weekly as police officers portrayed themselves as young children online. While this deterred many would-be child rapists, they simply found new resources that were less monitored by adults. Within a few years, the majority of children using location-based chat rooms were actually police officers looking for predators. This gave the appearance of solving the problem, but it only forced the molesters to be more creative and cautious. Arrests of online child solicitors occur every day; however, they only account for a small portion of those looking for children online. It is the responsibility of everyone, including parents, to protect children from these crimes. We believe that an understanding of the common avenues used by child sex offenders will help identify inappropriate behavior. We will present this information by the age groups of preschoolers, preteens, and teens.

The youngest group, preschoolers, is the hardest for pedophiles to target. Much of their online activity is monitored and they are seldom alone without parental supervision. Predators who are attracted to this age range often possess an urge toward these children that they cannot control. The majority of these attacks will occur after some type of legitimate physical interaction has taken place. This could be a friend of the family, a family member, or an acquaintance through an outside organization. They tend to be friendly with the parents in order to build up trust to be left alone with a child. The most common digital interaction is light grooming through shared computer use. Predators tend to offer to teach children of this age how to use computers and introduce them to games and instant messaging. Parents are usually aware of this activity, and we encourage them to keep a close eye on the interactions.

The second group, preteens, is the most likely to experience their first solicitation from an online stranger. This group is the most naïve and trusting of others. They have not been exposed to much adult content through various mediums such as television and the Internet. They tend to respond to any communication received online out of curiosity and politeness. These children need your full attention.

In the early days of the Internet, predators spent many hours grooming preteens online within various chat rooms and direct messaging. Pedophiles would contact any children within an online area and begin asking simple questions such as, "What is your favorite type of music?" and, "Do you have any brothers or sisters?" They would document the answers and use that information in later conversations. They could then begin a post by talking about a new song from the group that a child liked or make a comment about the difficulties of growing up with brothers and sisters. Predators possessed a craft of recycling any input from a child into a customized conversation that excited the child. In one of Michael's arrests, the offender spent an entire month grooming a child before meeting in real life.

Today, this grooming is not necessary. Our use of social networks has removed any unknowns about a child. A Facebook page will disclose every television, music, or movie interest of a child. A Twitter profile discloses the school attended and daily schedule of activities. Instagram posts identify friends and fashion styles of the victim. Overall, we have made it much easier for a predator to obtain all necessary personal details of a child in order to begin an assault through online conversation.

The most common avenue an attacker will take toward preteens is through their social network profiles. During an interview with a man in his 50s under arrest for luring a 12-year-old girl to an isolated park before molesting her, Michael asked why he had picked that specific girl as the victim. The predator said he had gone to Facebook, searched for girls who went to a nearby middle school, identified those that "liked" some type of alcoholic beverage, and offered them free alcohol in exchange for meeting him at the park. She was the first to accept his offer.

These stories seem far-fetched to many parents, but they are such common news that they often receive little attention in the media. At the time of this writing, news reports announced three separate incidents where adults raped 12-year-old girls that they met through Facebook. All of these occurred within five days. In one, a man groomed the girl for weeks before molesting her at her home. In another, a man flew 400 miles to meet the child he had been grooming for weeks. The third was even more horrendous.

A man tried to convince a 12-year-old victim to have sex with him, but she refused. The suspect then allegedly forcefully raped her at his home in Kyle, Texas. Several months later, the girl was found to be pregnant and an investigation began. The girl told authorities she only had sex one time and that was with the suspect. The child also said the suspect pursued her online for months, offering her money at one point, but she refused to go back to his home.

Our motive for sharing these stories is not to make your stomach turn. It is to highlight the necessity that parents become involved in their preteen's online activities. We believe this is two-fold. First, continuous conversations about the dangers of the Internet are vital. Over half of Michael's investigations into preteen sexual assaults from online encounters revealed parents who had never talked with their child about online safety. Second, parents should monitor all public information visible on their child's account, as explained previously.

The last group, teens, receive the majority of unwanted online solicitation from child molesters. This is not likely due to an attraction to this specific age range. Instead, it is due to a higher chance that a child in this age range will participate in a sexual encounter without notifying a parent. This group needs the most monitoring. We will outline the most common ways that children get entangled in these situations, and will discuss proper reporting in the next chapter.

In today's landscape, predators are usually after one of two things from teens: sexual encounters or child pornography. The routes taken to achieve their desires vary drastically. While attempts to obtain nude photos of young victims is more prevalent, unreported sexual activity between children and adult strangers is still shockingly high. We will tackle "sexting" and "sextortion" first.

"Sexting" is a relatively new word that typically refers to sex-related or nude digital photos taken with a cellular phone and shared online or through private communications. While most sexting occurs on phones through direct communication, only a small portion becomes publicly visible on the Internet. Sexting is not illegal when photos are shared between consenting adults; however, when minors are involved, sexual-exploitation and child-pornography laws become relevant. Regardless of the criminal implications, there can be significant psychological consequences. This is especially true when coercion is involved, or if consensual sexting between two people is later shared without consent.

Most sexting occurs between two people familiar with each other in the real world. They have existing relationships through school or other activities. They are likely to be similar in age; however, this can still violate child pornography laws. If a 15-year-old girl sends a nude photo of herself to a 15-year-old boy, they have both committed crimes. She could be charged with distribution of child pornography and he could face charges of possession of child pornography. While this type of prosecution is rare, it does happen occasionally.

There is a broad range of motivations behind sexting. For some, it is digital flirting, attention seeking, or an aspect of young dating relationships. For others, it is a gateway to blackmail and extortion. This type of behavior is commonly referred to as "sextortion." This term generally refers to the crime of extortion involving sex-related digital photos. Extortion victimizes someone by demanding money, property, sex, or some other service from the person and threatening to harm him or her if the demand is not met. When digital photos are involved, the threat is often embarrassment or reputation damage through exposure or distribution of the person's photos. The following is a typical example of sextortion from a known offender.

John, a 15-year-old student, sends a text to Jane, another 15-year-old student at the same school. He is flirtatious and shows interest in Jane through several dozen text messages. He eventually asks her for a topless photo, and promises to not show anyone else. She declines and he offers to send her a nude photo of himself. He locates a random pornographic image of a male on the Internet and forwards it to her. He pressures her into returning the action and claims that she owes him a photo. She gives in and sends a topless photo to John.

John now has something to use against Jane. He tells her to send a completely nude photo of herself, and she refuses. He tells her that if she does not comply, he will send the original photo of her to everyone at school and it will ruin her reputation. Jane concedes and sends the full nude photo. John now forces her to send new photos weekly and threatens to send copies of all images to her parents if she does not comply. Jane believes that she is completely stuck in this situation and has no recourse. This scenario occurs in real life daily for many teens. The following is a typical example of sextortion from a stranger.

Ted, a 50-year-old man identifies the Facebook page of Tina, a 15-year-old girl who lives in a nearby city. He begins an online conversation with her and identifies himself as a boy her age. He sends photos of a boy across the country that he located on another random Facebook page. As in the previous example, he requests nude photos and shares inappropriate images of a boy her age, claiming it is him. After she reluctantly sends an image, he begins the same process of demanding more photos, threatening to deliver copies of previous images to her parents. This cycle continues with other random girls with whom he begins communicating.

Children are often reluctant to tell even trusted adults about sexting or sextortion for a number of reasons. The primary reason is fear about potential outcomes. By reporting a peer, they feel they could make their situation much worse. They fear they could be judged by their friends, disciplined by adults, or have their bully retaliate in worse ways. Many young people have been told by the aggressors that they could face criminal charges if authorities get involved. While this is possible, it is extremely rare. Children are always considered victims in these incidents.

Teens are targeted online more than any other age group. While sexting and sextortion cases are growing more rapidly than sexual assaults, an alarming number of physical attacks are occurring after an online encounter with a stranger. As stated earlier, predators possess confidence while hidden behind a computer screen. They can communicate virtually with dozens of potential victims at the same time, only needing one of them to agree to a meeting. While social network profiles often lead pedophiles to their victims, it is the private communication that has the most concern.

Attackers will often use instant messaging services through Facebook, Snapchat, and other outlets to communicate directly with a victim. If Twitter is the environment, direct messages (DMs) will be sent instead of public tweets. These conversations are not visible to anyone outside of the participants. This presents a huge problem to parents as there is no easy way of monitoring this content. Predators know not to leave incriminating evidence on a child's profile and often refuse to create any public associations with the victim. This often presents a false sense of security when a parent sees no suspicious behavior when viewing the account.

This is precisely the reason that many parents insist on complete access to their child's mobile devices and online accounts. Knowing the screen lock code to the mobile device will allow you to open any apps and peruse previous and current conversations. Accessing online accounts with a child's user name and password allows you to view pending private messages with the intent of identifying inappropriate relationships. We have found that a child simply knowing that his or her parent has the ability to see private content greatly reduces the risk of inappropriate activity. This is regardless of whether the parent is actually investigating the account. Many parents believe, even if it is a bluff, that telling children about their ability to access communications is an effective deterrent. We tend to agree.

Lately, it is not only pedophiles that need to be a concern of parents. It is also the abundance of malicious hackers who illegally access and expose sensitive content created and stored by your child. Some are classmates of your teen seeking any data that could be used as part of bullying tactics. Others are strangers located several countries away from your child hoping to use the teen's popularity to deliver spam messages to millions of recipients. Instead of focusing on the multiple reasons why hackers will target your child's accounts, let's focus on solutions. While the following tips are applicable to everyone's online accounts, parents should take a moment to verify their child's information is secure.

- Assign a secure password to every account that your child accesses and document this for your own use. A secure password has at least eight digits and contains letters, numbers, and at least one special character.

- Do not repeat the password used for your child's email account within any social network. Hackers will attempt to log into an email account with the password stolen from a social network. If the hacker gets access to a child's email account, he or she can reset every other password used.

- Many online accounts allow a password reset after successfully answering a series of security questions that were provided during the creation of the account. These questions and answers are usually very generic and the data can be found online. Some security questions request the child's best friend's name, school mascot, or street on which they reside. These answers can all be obtained online or simply guessed by a culprit. Revisit these security options and choose more discreet questions and answers.

Finally, some children will "hack" the computers at a school with the intention of stealing login credentials of the kids that use them. This is usually conducted by installing a software or hardware key logger on each computer. Software key loggers are similar to viruses that record every key typed by each user. The suspect can then later retrieve these details and access private accounts. The hardware versions plug into the back of the computer and the keyboard is then plugged into the key logger. The suspect later retrieves the piece of hardware and extracts the keys typed by all users. The lesson to teach your child is to avoid supplying personal login credentials on any untrusted computers. Your child may be required to use school computers as part of their learning, but not to access email, Facebook, Twitter, or other personal networks. This may seem harsh for some parents or children. Only you can decide the appropriate level of security for your family.

A Question from a Parent

Rusty Edwards: I work at a children's home and I would love to teach parents how to protect their children once and for all. If banks and corporations with billions of dollars can't keep their own information from getting hacked, how do we protect the stuff our kids put online?

Amber's Answer: I believe that quite simply we cannot. Parents must always assume that all of the "private" things children share with their friends are public. While you and I might not be able to find it, a predator will always know the tricks. We must teach children that everything said or posted online is public, regardless of any privacy settings. I once gave the following advice at a high school presentation while discussing online content: "Before pressing the send button, assume that your grandmother will be given a copy. If that causes hesitation, delete the message."

Michael's Predator Timeline

I began investigating Internet crimes against children in 1998. The methods that predators used to lure children into harmful situations then was fairly basic and straightforward. Today, pedophiles must embrace the latest technology in order to keep up with child victims while staying undetected by law enforcement. The following represents the changes in my investigations and prosecutions of online predators over an eighteen-year period.

1998-2000: Pedophiles begin using the Internet to communicate with potential child victims online. Yahoo Messenger offers a location-based option that allows people to chat with others near their current location. Rooms with cities as titles, such as "St. Louis," attract both children and predators in mass numbers. Several arrests are made while police conduct online stings, portraying themselves as children. Pedophiles openly solicit these undercover cops offering money and alcohol in exchange for sex with children as young as twelve. My average amount of time online before I was solicited was under three minutes.

2001-2003: News of the chat room sex stings gain national media attention, but predators continue to use this medium as an avenue to solicit children. Child pornography websites appear on rare occasion, but an abundance of illegal images appear within the Usenet system. Collectors of child pornography upload and download the files openly with little risk of getting caught. Internet service providers shut down the illicit groups when identified, but new repositories populate the market quicker than those found can be disabled.

2004-2006: The television show To Catch A Predator debuts and exposes the huge underworld of online pedophiles. This creates a scare within the illegal community and many of the worst offenders refrain from the most used chat rooms. The social network MySpace gains incredible popularity with teenagers, and predators take notice. In years prior, a pedophile would need to "groom" a child for days or weeks in order to identify his or her musical tastes and interests. This occurred over numerous chat sessions. The presence of a social media profile eliminated this task and allowed the suspect to conduct a much more focused attack against the child. Knowing intimate details about the victim allows the suspect to mirror the child's interests in hopes of quickly advancing the relationship.

2007-2008: Peer to peer technology emerges as a new avenue for pedophiles to exchange child pornography. Simple programs such as eDonkey and LimeWire facilitate easy file sharing between strangers in real-time. Police conduct numerous online stings by downloading known child pornography images and videos, and track the offender's Internet Protocol (IP) address to the residence where the computer is located.

2009-2011: Predators begin infiltrating online video games as a way to meet children under the radar of law enforcement. As kids connect over the Internet and play first-person shooter games, pedophiles join the ranks and verbally communicate with potential victims over connected headsets. This presents new challenges to law enforcement as this activity was not well monitored or documented.

2012-2014: Mobile apps such as Snapchat increase in popularity with young people. The allure of a "disappearing" message entices children into sharing nude "selfies" with complete strangers. Predators commonly blackmail children for additional images or threaten to share the uploaded content with parents. The use of Voice Over Internet Protocol (VOIP) telephone numbers create headaches for investigators trying to identify the suspects.

2015-2016: Overall, predators still use all of the avenues mentioned previously. The data gleaned from social network profiles combined with the convenience of simple apps creates a dangerous environment. The protections of encrypted communications and anonymous Internet connections makes prosecution extremely difficult. Children are constantly bombarded with unwanted sexual solicitation and most instances are never reported to parents.

This timeline may be a bit depressing for the concerned parents reading this book. During my career, I had the unfortunate obligation to inform numerous parents that their child had been victimized by an online predator. There was one common theme within all of these conversations. The parents simply did not understand the technology being used by the child. They were not aware of the numerous ways that predators were able to communicate with the child victim right under their noses. The simple steps that you are taking now in order to learn about these dangers puts you at a great advantage if a similar situation occurs within your family. You will now be better prepared.

Chapter Nine
Reporting Strategies

We hope that the parents reading this book will never need this chapter. For those who encounter inappropriate activity between a child and online attackers, it is vital to understand legal recourse, reporting options, and removal techniques. We will tackle each throughout this chapter and hope it can be used as a reference guide if your family encounters online trouble.

We should first define what is, and what is not, online criminal activity. While every state and country possesses its own laws regarding Internet crime, there are commonalities that exist. Overall, soliciting a minor for sex is always a crime, as is possession, distribution, and manufacture of child pornography. There is no grey area there and those crimes should be obvious to any police agency taking your report. What may not be obvious is the proper jurisdiction for reporting. Overall, the local police department that provides services to the residential area of the child victim is the appropriate first contact. This department should take the report and begin the investigation. If the suspect lives in a nearby community, the originating department will likely maintain the case and prosecute from their jurisdiction. Child sex crimes are unique in that the location of the victim often maintains jurisdiction regardless of the location of the offender. This is not usually the case in other types of digital crimes such as identity theft or unlawful use of a credit card.

Many parents become frustrated when they report an incident to police, but nothing can be done legally about the situation. This happens often when one student harasses another child online, but does not cross the line of criminal activity. Common examples include the following actions by an offender.

- Creating a fake social network page in the name of another person.
- Posting slanderous statements about someone online.
- Sending numerous unwanted messages to the victim.

While these are all mean and inappropriate, they are not illegal in most areas. The mean kids in your history class who made fun of others on the playground have been replaced with online bullies that can spread hatred to hundreds of people within seconds from a computer. Computer crime laws cannot keep up with the numerous ways that people facilitate digital abuse. Another confusing area is the presence of online threats. Most states require a threat of physical harm in order to classify the action as a crime. As an example, the following statements from one child to another would be considered crimes in most areas.

I'm going to kill you.
I'm going to beat you up tomorrow.
I'm going to hurt you.
I'm going to have someone else hurt you.

However, the following would usually not be considered criminal statements, even in a juvenile court.

I hate you.
I wish you were dead.
I hope something bad happens to you.
I'm going to tell everyone lies about you.

Overall, there is a line that must be crossed in order to separate hateful conversation from criminal activity. There must be a threat of violence to clearly qualify for a criminal complaint. If your situation meets the legal requirements for prosecution in your area, the next step is to notify authorities. Previously, we mentioned contacting your local police department. If you live in an urban area, there is very likely a computer crimes division that is well-versed in these situations. If you live in a rural area, you may encounter an officer who has not been trained in computer crime investigation. He or she may not have the resources necessary to properly prosecute this type of case. When that happens, escalate the complaint one level until you receive the response you deserve, as we describe below.

In the United States, most local police departments are within a county that has its own police agency. These county Sheriff's departments are usually equipped for various computer crime investigations. If you are still met with a lack of understanding about your case, move on to the state police for your area. Within these three options, you are practically guaranteed to find one that has completed similar cyber investigations. As a worst case scenario, you can report your incident to the Internet Crime Complaint Center (IC3) at their website **www.ic3.gov**. The only hesitation in completely relying on this service is that complaints take time to be assigned to an investigator in your area. It could easily be 30 days before you receive a response.

In Canada, cybercrimes against youth can be reported to municipal law enforcement agencies that will either utilize internal subject-matter resources for online investigations or engage the assistance of specialized Internet investigative units with provincial or federal partners. Canadians are also encouraged to report online crimes against youth on a national tip line at **www.cybertip.ca**. Tips may be submitted anonymously and are forwarded to local law enforcement and child welfare services. In addition, informational resources and advice on reporting cyberbullying as well as other crimes against youth are available on the **DEAL.org** website, which is operated by the Youth Engagement Section of the Royal Canadian Mounted Police.

If you cannot determine whether your situation qualifies as a criminal complaint, we encourage you to still contact your local police. They may be aware of additional resources available to you. Many agencies possess a school resource officer who is assigned to assist with these complicated situations.

Online Content Removal

In 2015, Michael was contacted by a young woman who was suffering from a bad case of online stalking. Her ex-boyfriend constantly harassed her and her new boyfriend online. He posted malicious content on various websites and referenced them both by full name. He had posted so much content that some of it had made it to the front page of a Google search. At one point, the first result after searching her name was a pornographic video fictitiously claiming to be her. Fellow students were now searching her name in order to view the video that they believed to be her. She had enough and wanted to take action.

These cases are sometimes difficult to tackle because of laws that protect free speech. However, we believe that one has a right to take advantage of laws and policies in order to protect a reputation. The goal was to eliminate all malicious content from the first page of both Google and Bing searches of her name. The following highlights the successes and failures, and may provide assistance if you encounter a similar situation.

The first website on her Google and Bing search results was a revenge pornography page. It displayed a pornographic video of an unknown female (not the victim) who appeared to be asleep on a bed. An unknown man (not the suspect) then sexually molests the woman while she sleeps. It should be noted that this video was likely staged and the female actress was probably a willing participant. These consensual videos have become popular on commercial pornography websites. The title of the video on this page included the victim's full name. The comments made several references to her, the new boyfriend, and her family. It is assumed that the former boyfriend wanted the world to think that the woman in the video was the young woman (victim). They did appear very similar physically.

Removing this first link was relatively simple. Michael first navigated to the official Google revenge porn reporting page at the following website.

https://support.google.com/websearch/troubleshooter/3111061

He selected the following options, each of which appeared after each subsequent question posed by Google.

What do you want to do? *Remove information you see in Google Search*
The information I want removed is: *In Google's search results and on a website*
Have you contacted the site's webmaster? *Yes, but they haven't responded*
I want to remove: *A pornographic site that contains a full name*
Does the page contain pornographic content? *Yes*
Does a full name appear on the website without your permission? *Yes*
Does the page violate Google's Webmaster Quality Guidelines? *Yes*

He then supplied an email address that he created for the victim, the full name of the victim as it appeared on the web page, the address of the Google result page linking to the video, and the address of the actual video page. He submitted the request and moved on to Bing.

He navigated to Bing's simple "Report Content to Microsoft" website located online at the following website.

https://support.microsoft.com/getsupport?oaspworkflow=start_1.0.0.0&w fname=capsub&productkey=RevengePorn

He provided the victim's name as it appeared on the video page, the exact address of the page, confirmation that the victim did not consent to the posting, and a digital signature.

He received a response from Bing within 24 hours, and the link was removed. Google responded over 15 days later and they also removed the link. Both cited their revenge porn policies and gave no resistance to the removal. While the female in the video was not the victim, we believe that identifying the victim as the participant warranted this type of link-removal submission. Interestingly, neither service specifically asked if the requestor was actually in the pornographic video. They only required that the requestor's name be included on the page.

At this point, the Bing results page was fairly clean. The first page included legitimate social network pages under the control of the victim. However, Google was a different story. The suspect had created a post on a popular revenge pornography web forum where he linked to the previously mentioned video. Technically, this video was not present on the website, only the mention of it and a direct link. This forum post was now the number one result when searching the victim's name. This page made several references to her full name and identified her in the inappropriate video. Michael submitted this page through the same Google reporting page and waited. He was denied the request because the page did not contain any actual pornography. The direct link did not satisfy the requirements of their takedown policy.

Michael took drastic action that would not be appropriate for all situations. This web forum allows any members to post comments about the videos. He created a new member account anonymously, and submitted a comment on the page in question. In this comment, he embedded a small image that displayed a single frame of the video. He resubmitted the request to Google and the link was removed nine days later. The rest of the results on the first page of her Google search were legitimate websites that she approved.

The takeaway from this situation is two-fold. First, you can request that Google and Bing remove some types of content from their search results pages. There must be some type of danger to the child in order for them to comply. The second lesson is that you can combat resistance from these services by creatively resubmitting your request. In this example, Michael actually added to the problem, but also helped qualify the link for removal in the same step. If you identify any malicious content about your child while searching Google or Bing, ask them to remove it through the previously mentioned websites. If you locate any harmful information about your child within social networks, the following details will assist with removal.

Facebook

If you want to report something that goes against Facebook's Community Standards, such as nudity, hate speech, or violence, use the "Report" link near the post, photo, or comment to report it to them. If you want to report something that goes against the Community Standards but you don't have an account, or can't see the content because someone blocked you, complete the form at the following website.

https://www.facebook.com/help/contact/274459462613911

Twitter

You can report tweets, direct messages, and account profiles that are in violation of the Twitter rules or their terms of service. Violations you can report include abusive or harmful content and impersonation.

To report an individual tweet:

- Navigate to the tweet you would like to report.
- Click the "More" icon (•••).
- Select "Report."
- Select "They're being abusive or harmful."
- Provide additional information about the issue you're reporting.

To report a direct message:

- Click into the direct message conversation.
- Hover over the message and click the "report" icon when it appears.
- Select "Mark as abusive" and click again to confirm.

To report an account profile:

- Open the profile you would like to report.
- Select the gear icon.
- Select "Report" and then "They're being abusive or harmful."
- Provide additional information about the issue you're reporting.

Instagram

You can report photos, videos, comments, or profiles on Instagram that are bullying or harassing others. Navigate to the following website and provide the details.

https://help.instagram.com/contact/584460464982589

YouTube

YouTube provides an online interface for reporting harmful content that is associated with your child. Visit the following website and complete the six steps required.

https://support.google.com/youtube/answer/142443

Summary

As we mentioned previously, most of the major online services have detailed information on their sites about how to report content for removal. However, be warned, it can be a time-consuming process. You should also now have a better understanding in terms of what is, and what is not, online criminal activity. Although bullying may be something that you are inclined to report to authorities, remember to closely look at the example we showcase above that identifies if that bullying does in fact include a threat of physical harm. Your recourse in most bullying cases that do not include such a threat will probably involve a number of people, including other parents, other kids, and in many cases, your child's school. **Stopbullying.gov** has an excellent section on its website that details how all of these parties can work together, explaining that "Research shows that school administrators, such as principals, can play a powerful role in bullying prevention. They can inspire others and maintain a climate of respect and inclusion. But a principal cannot do it alone." Again, we stress how a community solution is often the best approach. In the next chapter, we'll expand on how parents can spearhead these conversations. Plus, we'll talk about online etiquette and how all adults need to embrace their position in the home as positive role models online. We'll also discuss tips to approach your children if you're concerned about their safety and security, and how to maintain an open dialogue.

A Question from a Parent

Arden Llewellyn: How do we know how far to trust our kids? Even with a loving, trusting home environment, kids can be led by those outside the household into using apps that hide folders, text messages, and pics. So even if you make an agreement with the kids that you need to know their passwords on all devices until 18, you may not be able to find all of their activities.

Amber's Answer: You are absolutely right. Although we have outlined some excellent ways to stay on top of what your kids are doing on Twitter, Facebook, Instagram, and within other apps, none of this is 100 percent guaranteed to solve the problems that you are facing as a family. In terms of how much you can trust your child, every kid is different and this is a question only his or her parent can answer. If you are seriously worried about their safety in terms of the content they are hiding from you, you might have to remove access to technology altogether and review the reporting strategies we outlined in Chapter Nine.

Chapter Ten
Parent Patrol

Parents often dream up creative ideas to deal with their kids and their experiences online. While we understand that this is sometimes a necessity, and we support it when it makes sense, there are too many instances when adults choose the wrong tactics to teach their children valuable digital lessons. One of the most famous examples includes a Colorado mother and her daughter. Back in 2014, Kira Hudson decided she needed to teach her 12-year-old a lesson about why she was too young to use social media. She took a photo of her little girl holding a sign that said, "Mom is trying to show me how many people can see a picture once it's on the Internet." The concept seems innocent enough, but here is an example of how an experiment, which many people online later called public shaming, went seriously wrong.

Very quickly, the photo was posted on 4chan, an image board website consisting of mostly anonymous users. To teach this mom a lesson, they tracked down Hudson's contact information, prank called her, and sent pizzas to her home. They also mocked up the original image with a new message, "Maybe you shouldn't use your daughter as an experiment to prove your point. Just an idea." Hudson indeed proved her point to her daughter, but perhaps not in the way she originally intended.

Although this is a mild form of public shaming, there have been numerous stories in the media about other parents taking things even further. There is a popular Instagram and Tumblr account that showcases very young children in various states of tantrums. The mom of four who created this, Kristen Howerton, told *Redbook Magazine* that she launched these channels with the sarcastic hashtag #assholeparent to demonstrate how disappointed kids can get about minor, unimportant things (such as a parent putting cilantro on a two year old's burrito). At first glance, it's hard not to chuckle at some of the images. However, there is a strong argument that this behavior is not setting a good example for the next generation of Internet users. When you think about the future of these kids in the photos online, you start to realize that sarcasm aside, posting these is actually an #assholeparent move.

In this chapter, we'll discuss proper online etiquette for everyone in the family. While we've addressed how kids are using the Internet, parents also have an opportunity to improve their own posting habits and set a better example for their children. We will also explain how to regularly search information online about your child, whether it's their real name or a user name. Finally, we will share the best strategies to talk to your children about everything you've learned about Internet safety and security in this book and beyond.

Online Etiquette

If you think back to Facebook's launch in 2004, kids born in that year are now coming into their teen years. Chances are, their parents posted many of their childhood photos online. These kids make up the first group of people who are entering the most difficult years in their lives with the possibility of hundreds of potentially embarrassing photos on the Internet (photos that their own parents posted!). Researchers at the University of Washington led a recent parent-child study that indicates that "children ages 10 to 17 'were really concerned' about the ways parents shared their children's lives online, while their parents were far less worried. About three times more children than parents thought there should be rules about what parents shared on social media."

Many of them explained that they didn't like their parents' social media habits. Today, these moms and dads are struggling to teach their kids good online etiquette, and it's no wonder. If Mom or Dad doesn't respect a child's privacy online, it's difficult for the child to act any differently. Again, this is a family problem that needs a family solution. Here are three online etiquette rules to follow that can help. Consider posting these rules in a public place in the house, beginning when your youngest kids are first going online, to reinforce their importance. Again, parents must also follow suit to make good social media choices.

Avoid oversharing: For both parents and kids, it's key to emphasize that while sharing on social media is OK, oversharing is not. To avoid oversharing means a few different things. It means that no one posts photos or videos of another member of the family (or friends) without asking first. It means no one shares any photos of the home that could easily reveal the address (the same applies to school). It also means no sharing personal information that you wouldn't want someone else to find online. These same rules apply when you're outside the home.

Avoid overreacting: There is a tendency for all social media users to quickly respond to messages, often acting impulsively and saying things that are hurtful. It's a good idea for all online networking users to step away from the phone, tablet, or computer if something is upsetting them. Take a 15-minute break and come back to the conversation; chances are, at this point, you will feel less anger after a mini digital time-out.

Avoid bullying: While piling on is often a common thing to do online, avoid participating in all bullying scenarios. While we often worry about kids as victims of bullies, we spend far too little time ensuring that our kids aren't the ones doing the bullying. For this rule, it's also critical to share a family plan in terms of what to do if you witness bullying (such as keeping a record of it and sharing it with an adult).

There are more rules that apply in terms of promoting positive online etiquette. We've gone through many of these throughout the book, such as not talking to strangers, not using your real name as your user name, and not assuming that conversations are ever private.

Talking to Your Kids

After you've established online etiquette rules, it's important to consider how to effectively talk to your kids if they break these rules. For most parents, this is the most difficult part of the job. While your preschoolers and preteens may be more inclined to engage in these conversations, teens may be a more difficult audience. Alyson Schafer, parenting expert and author of *Honey, I Wrecked the Kids*, has some advice to deal with this age group.

"As with any important conversation with our teens, we have to approach the subject so that they perceive us as their caring ally, rather than the controlling parent," she says. "If you try to control a teen, they will find ways to rebel or sneak around your rules. Tweens and teens decide for themselves whose influence they will take. If your relationship with your teen is strong and close, then when you share a concern you have for them and their well-being. They will be receptive to your perspective and open to your wisdom."

Schafer also recommends that you lose the lecturing, nagging, or threats (sure, it might be your first instinct, but it will not end well). She also explains that a good conversation is a bit like holding a mirror up to your teens; encouraging them to explain how they're feeling; and helping them to thoroughly process their thoughts. She adds that it's important to ask Internet safety and security questions out of curiosity, again, instead of anger. To build on this curiosity angle in terms of dealing with these delicate conversations, she says you should consider the following four steps:

Point out what you are seeing. Comments like this work: *I have noticed you are spending more time in your room now than you ever have before. Have you noticed that?*

Ask how they are feeling about their time online. Questions like this work: *How do you feel about the amount of time you are on your own and isolated from your family?*

Ask what they make of the situation. Questions like this work: *What is your best guess at what's going on?*

Ask if you can share what you've been thinking and feeling from your perspective. Statements like this will get a more reasoned response: *I am worried that while you may love your time with friends, and you're growing new branches in the world, but you may not be putting in the time to keep your roots alive - and they're important for your long term stability and growth too. We've been missing you and wonder if you too have been feeling like you're drifting from us?*

Again, parents often point their anger directly at their own children. In regard to how to keep your child safe and secure online, she asks that Moms and Dads reframe every conversation on this topic so that it is an "I" message rather than a "you" message. While we spoke above about online etiquette rules for kids, this is one for parents. Schafer says statements like these express your feelings, so you leave lecturing, nagging, or threats out of the equation:

- I feel concerned you're building bad habits.
- I feel sad when I see you sad over the conversation that upset you.
- I feel worried that your school work is being compromised and that you'll be upset with yourself at report card time.

She explains, "These statements will be heard better than "you" statements that judge, lay blame, point the finger." An example of "you" statements that will inevitably lead to defensive responses are as follows:

- You are on the computer too much.
- You never put that thing down!
- You're being rude - look at me when we talk.

In all of her work, Schafer recommends practical solutions for busy parents. With years of research, clinical, and field experience as a therapist, she's been successful in teaching parents across North America on how to deal with kids' poor online choices. She always recommends working together with your child, something we've reinforced throughout this book, to create common goals.

"Once you've identified the growth inhibiting habit, create common goals with your child so they feel like a stakeholder in moving towards a more healthy relationship with technology," Schafer says. "Suggest ways that you can help build up better boundaries with them. Get their buy-in. Try small experiments in change to see if the ideas are helping. Baby steps, empathy, support are all critical. Your approach should be both firm on upholding agreements, but be friendly and warm in your manner. If you decide that parking the technology 30 minutes or more before bedtime, as suggested by sleep experts, you can pack up their iPad by saying 'Sorry, I know it's hard to be the first of your group to say good night, but this is what we agreed to try for one week. Let's give this a good try before we decide if we keep this rule."

Finally, she emphasizes one of the most important goals of this book. What we're trying to do is to teach parents and kids how to use technology responsibly. In terms of one last piece of advice to cement this outcome with a child, she suggests the following wording:

"If you can show me you can manage your tech use responsibly, then I won't need to manage it. But if you find that too difficult, I can step in and help you with that, and you can try again on your own in a while. But tech does need to be managed."

While some parents may feel as though getting too involved in a child's online habits equates to spying on your kids, it's quite the opposite. If you simply turn a blind eye, you are neglecting to help them with one of the most potentially important tools in today's world.

Child Background Check

Parents should occasionally take a moment to identify the types of personal information present about their children. This is not a one-time event. Some parents check up on their children daily or weekly while others take a peek every other month. Your strategy will vary based on the level of exposure of your child. We recommend the following methods in order to conduct thorough, yet quick "background checks" on your own child.

Search Engines

The first basic step is to identify the standard information available online about your child within search engines. In order to properly search for the information, you will need to do more than a standard Google search. Search engines will help you tremendously, but you will need to provide specific instruction when conducting your queries. For the first group of searches, assume that the following information describes your child.

John Williams
1212 Main Street
Houston, TX
713-555-1234
johnnyw@gmail.com

Searching "John Williams" will likely not be productive. Even if it were a unique name, the results would include spam and websites that provided no valuable information. Instead, conduct the following search including the quotation marks.

"John Williams" "Houston"

This query instructs the search engine to locate web pages that have exactly John Williams and Houston on the same page. This will eliminate many unwanted pages that do not contain relevant information. If your child's name is generic, such as John Williams, you may still be bombarded with unwanted results. Try the following search.

"John Williams" "1212 Main"

This query instructs the search engine to locate web pages that have exactly John Williams and 1212 Main on the same page. This will likely display pages that announce your child's home address to the world. You should also search the following example to locate pages that display your home telephone number.

"John Williams" "555" "1234"

This query instructs the search engine to locate web pages that have exactly John Williams and 555 and 1234 on the same page. The two sets of numbers were searched separately in case the target websites did not use a hyphen (-) when separating the numbers. These queries will locate online content that references your child's name and home address. Additional searches should be conducted based on the name and associations such as a school, interests, or organizations. Create your own custom queries based on the following example searches.

"Michael Bazzell" "Unionville High School"
"Michael Bazzell" "Marching Band"
"Michael Bazzell" "Debate Club"

The quotation marks in the above searches are vital to the queries. They inform the search engine to only look for exactly what is presented. This will prevent Google and others from adjusting your search in order to "help" you. Each search engine that you use will likely give different results. You may want to try variations of your child's name. If his first name is "Michael" you will also want to search "Mike." If you do not receive any results, you may want to repeat the search without the quotation marks. After you have identified the various websites that display your child's residence and telephone information, you should identify services that are connected to an email address. To obtain accurate results of your email search, quotation marks must be used. An exact search such as "johnnyw@gmail.com" on Google should be helpful.

Alternative Search Engines

There is no lack of search engines that could be used. While Google and Bing are the two main players, there are many other specialty engines that display results the others miss. The following is a list of recommended search engines for your background check of your child.

Google.com   Exalead.com   Bing.com/images
Bing.com   Groups.google.com   Qwant.com
Yahoo.com   News.google.com
Yandex.com   Google.com/images

Michael's Hacks

All-In-One Search Tool

The website IntelTechniques (**inteltechniques.com/osint/user.html**) maintains a page that will allow you to conduct a single query across multiple websites in one click. This is our preferred method when conducting a background check on a child. This website will present many search fields that will allow you to execute a query on various services. The last search field at the bottom will allow you to execute any query on all of the listed services. Figure 10.01 displays this page. Clicking the "Submit All" button will open a new tab for each service.

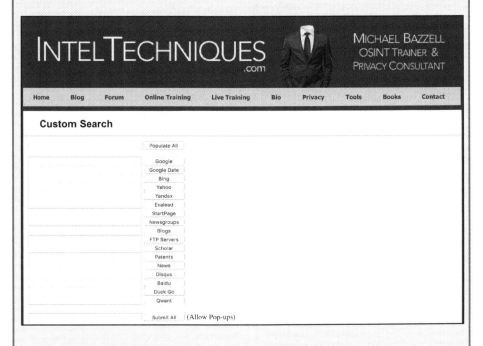

Figure 10.01: A custom search page on IntelTechniques.com.

User Names

You may wish to search for any social networks that your child has visible on the Internet. You probably found relevant Facebook and Twitter pages, but how many networks did he or she join and abandon when they lost popularity? We often forget about MySpace, Friendster, and other profiles that are no longer in use. Often, those profiles are still visible and may contain personal information. The easiest way to discover any accounts that may still be lingering is to search by your child's user name. Since kids usually use the same user name for numerous accounts, you may look at known social networks for a hint. You may want to search your child's Twitter name, Facebook profile name, or the first part of an email account. If your child's personal email address is "michaelb911@yahoo.com," you may want to search for only "michaelb911." Locating all possible network profiles can be a daunting task. Fortunately, we have services to assist us.

KnowEm

KnowEm (**knowem.com**) is one of the most comprehensive search websites for user names. The main page provides a single search field which will immediately check for the presence of the supplied user name on the most popular social network sites. In the main page, a user name search provides information about the availability of that user name on the top 25 networks. If the network name is slightly transparent and the word "available" is stricken, that means there is a subject with a profile on that website using the supplied user name. When the website is not transparent and the word "available" is orange and underlined, there is not a user profile on that site with the supplied user name.

For your purposes, these "unavailable" indications suggest a visit to the site to locate your child's profile. The "Check over 500 more" link in the lower left corner of the page will open a new page that will search over 500 social networks for the presence of the supplied user name. These searches are completed by category, and the "blogging" category is searched automatically. Scrolling down this page will present 14 additional categories with a button next to each category title stating "check this category." This search can take some time. If your child has a unique user name that he or she likes to use, the search is well worth the time as you may uncover profiles on social networking sites you've never heard of before.

Location-Based Searches

You have now likely located the publicly available content associated with your child. This will often be easy to find because it is searchable by his or her name, address, or telephone number. However, there is often social network information that is defined by the location from where it was posted. Many services such as Twitter and Instagram embed the GPS coordinates of the user along with the posted content, as mentioned in previous chapters. This can quickly identify where a child lives or visits. Your child, friends, and family may not think about this type of technology and unintentionally compromise the entire family's privacy. You should consider conducting searches based on location as well as text. The easiest way to do this is through the service mentioned near the beginning of the book, Echosec.

Echosec

This simple website allows you to zoom to any location and query social network posts that were submitted from that location. Conduct the following steps to search your targeted area.

- Connect to **app.echosec.net** in your web browser.

- Either navigate through the interactive map or type your child's school address directly into the search box in the lower left.

- Click the "Select Area" button in the center bottom portion of the page. Draw a box around the target area and release the mouse.

- Navigate through any results displayed below the map.

The square icons within the map identify Twitter and Flickr posts by the location they were uploaded. This type of sharing can quickly disclose sensitive details. You might locate personal information that would have been difficult to find based on keyword searches alone. This can be a useful technique to find a child's account when they are unwilling to share it with you. This will only search recent Twitter posts. Repeat the search with other locations your child frequents (home address, friend's address, mall, etc.).

Checking Other Children

Many parents search for their child online and do not cross the boundary separating their own kid from others associated with him or her. Others conduct thorough queries on every friend of whom they are aware. Either is legal and available to anyone with an Internet connection. It is ultimately up to you on how to proceed. We stand in the middle on this issue. We believe that every parent should conduct multiple online searches in reference to their own child. We also believe that parents should expand this search to include other children when problems are detected. If you discover a bully is harassing your child and others online, we think that further searching into that child is appropriate.

We urge caution when searching for children outside of your own family. While not illegal, it may carry a negative feeling if discovered by another parent. Place yourself in their shoes. What if you found out that a parent you have never met was checking up on your own child? Many reading this book may have no objection to this, but others could be disturbed by these actions. Therefore, we encourage parents to consider another avenue.

Disclosing Results to Parents

After you have perfected your online search techniques, consider reaching out to other parents of children associated with your child. Disclose what you found, how you found it, and offer one of two services; teach parents how to replicate your efforts, or offer to conduct searches on their children. This seems to soften the blow instead of simply announcing details found about another child. We hope that you find other parents are as interested as you are with this topic. The next consideration is what to disclose to the kids.

There are two basic schools of thought on disclosure of online research into children. Some parents do not tell their kids about this new skill set and allow their children to continue posting sensitive details on the Internet. It allows those parents a peek into the most accurate portrayal of the everyday life of a child. Other parents choose to tell their children about their new talents as a deterrent toward future inappropriate activity. As usual, we stand somewhere in the middle.

If you discover absolutely no damaging information and everything appears normal in your child's online life, we believe this skill should be reserved and unannounced. If you find details that need to be immediately addressed, we feel that you should share your efforts with the child, offer to help repair the damages, and disclose that you will continue to monitor every aspect of his or her online life. After proving your successes with identification of inappropriate behavior, the deterrent will be obvious. Your child will never know if that next post will be read by you or not.

Social Network Privacy Settings

Most social networks provide an option to protect your child's personal details from the public. This is usually in the form of privacy settings that you can customize. These settings allow you to specify who can see the content of your child's profile. This can determine who can see his or her messages, photos, current location, employer, school information, friends, family, and other details. You can specify that either the public can see everything, or that certain details can only be viewed by people who your child has classified as "friends." Facebook also provides another option of "Friends of friends." This means that people your child does not know can see the information if they know someone who your child has classified as a friend. Modifying these settings to restrict who can see the data is advised. However, it can also create a false sense of security and encourage your child to post sensitive content. Here are a few things to consider about privacy settings.

These settings only prohibit the public from seeing the content. The content is still visible to the company that owns the social network. When you created the account, you agreed to a long list of legal terms called the terms of service. These terms probably discussed how the company that owns the social network can do whatever they want with the data that you provide. While these networks may be careful not to share your private data now, no one knows what will happen in the future.

Privacy settings can also be incredibly confusing. Some larger social networks may have dozens of privacy settings and hundreds of combinations of settings. This can make choosing the most private and secure options difficult. Privacy settings are subject to change. Facebook is notorious for updating its privacy policy to allow more and more of your data to become less and less private. Frequently, when the privacy policy changes many of your privacy settings will change. When these automatic changes occur, they will not be usually in the interest of protecting users' privacy. They will be to the benefit of the social network and will make as much of your child's information public and accessible as possible.

It is common to read in technology news sources about people who break into other people's accounts to steal information. Celebrities are continually having their accounts compromised by self-proclaimed "hackers" for both fun and profit. If someone wants your child's data bad enough, he or she will likely get it illegally.

Finally, there are many legal ways to retrieve data that is believed to be private. Michael has demonstrated during his law enforcement training how videos and photos from "hidden" Facebook profiles can be located through online tools and how the Twitter API can reveal personal details that are not visible on a person's profile page, including exact location. Many parents take a quick glance at their child's profile and are satisfied that only those with approved access can see the content. They are often wrong.

We believe that any time your child posts anything to the Internet, one must assume it is for public view. Even if the child has the privacy settings locked as tight as possible, you should accept that there is a possibility that someone else could get the data. If the content being uploaded to a private page would also be acceptable for public view, then one can proceed. However, if the inappropriate photos of your child would embarrass him or her if anyone but close friends saw it, one should not take the chance. Privacy settings will not always save you.

Content Removal

If you have looked at your child's profiles and have identified personal data that you no longer want on the Internet, you can remove it. There are too many different social networks to provide tailored instruction for the removal of specific information. The process is usually fairly easy. If you have trouble, an Internet search will give you the answers. Ultimately, any information that your child included in a profile can be removed, but this is only a bandage over the real problem. If you located any damaging details, there is likely much more available that you were unable to locate. Many teenaged children have no concern about privacy and the dangers of online information. Many will post hundreds of photos from their daily habits that will expose every intimate detail of their lives. Instead of patching the exposure that you find, we believe account deletion is a better option. When you approve, the child can always create a new account and abide by the guidelines that you present.

Account Deletion

By now, you may be considering completely removing all of your child's social networks. This process is not as easy as you would think. Social networks want the profiles and, more importantly, eyes on their advertisements. Facebook's home page does not inform you how to delete your account. Actually, no social network does this. It is very important to delete your accounts in a specific manner to ensure that the data is removed. The process to do this on several popular networks will be explained here.

Facebook

If your child's Facebook content is public, there are several data mining sites collecting everything that is posted including comments, photos, and friends. The first layer of privacy that you should implement is appropriate privacy settings. Recently, Facebook made this process much easier than before. After you log into the account, click on the "down arrow" in the upper right corner of the page. Choose the "Settings" option and select "Privacy." In the section called "Who can see my stuff?" you can edit your desired settings.

You will now have four choices of how you want to protect the data. The first choice, "Public," allows anyone to see all of the profile information. This is not advised. The second option, "Friends," allows only the people who your child has identified as friends to Facebook. This is a slightly more secure option. The third option of "Only me" is designed to make the posts completely private and only visible by your child. The last option allows you to customize different areas of the profile so that different people can see different types of content. We only recommend this for advanced Facebook users. If you are going to allow your child the use of Facebook, select the "Friends" option. More importantly, make sure that the subjects listed on the friends list are people your child really knows.

Many parents have decided to completely delete their child's Facebook profile. They have discovered that this process is not as easy as it should be.

Additionally, a Facebook account cannot be deleted right away. There is a "waiting period" of fourteen days. After the account is deleted, photos may remain on the Facebook servers for months or years. These photos are the legal property of Facebook. This may sound discouraging, but the sooner you begin deleting inappropriate information on Facebook, the better off you will be. If you are ready to pull the plug, the following are the proper steps.

- Log into the account and delete all of the content that you can. This includes all photos, messages, and interests.

- Navigate to **www.facebook.com/help/delete_account.**

- Click on the "Delete My Account" button. This will technically deactivate the account for two weeks. If your child logs into the account any time within that period, it could be reactivated.

- Your child will immediately receive an email from Facebook confirming the deletion request.

Twitter

Deleting your child's Twitter account is fairly straightforward. Go to your settings page. On the bottom of the account tab, there is a "Deactivate my account" link. Click it, and confirm. Before you take the easy route, we encourage you to consider a few things.

If your child has a Twitter profile with personal posts associated with it, there are dozens of websites that have collected all of the data and reproduced it. Deleting the account will not remove the posts that are replicated on third party websites. Before deleting the account, remove every message that your child has ever posted. Eventually, many of the third party websites that collect Twitter data will rescan the profile and update the messages that are displayed on their site. Often, this will overwrite the information that is currently displayed with the current messages, which will be none. We prefer this over simply deleting the account. Also, when you delete the account, someone can open up a new account with your child's profile name after 30 days. With this method, you still have control of the account; there are no personal messages associated with it; and sites that collect your Twitter posts will collect the empty profile. Active Twitter users often have thousands of messages on their account. Removing each message individually can be very time consuming. Instead, consider automatic message deletion options such as Twit Wipe (**twitwipe.com**) or Tweet Delete (**Tweetdelete.net**). These will do the work for you.

YouTube

The only way to delete your child's YouTube account is to delete the associated Google+ profile. Before you take this action, you should delete your child's YouTube Channels. These contain the videos, comments, messages, playlists, and history within the YouTube account. The following steps will allow you to remove these containers.

- Sign into your child's Google account and navigate to the website **youtube.com/account_advanced**.

- In the top right, click your child's account, then YouTube settings. Under the "Account Settings" select "Overview." Under each channel's name, select "Advanced."

- At the bottom of each channel, select "Delete channel" and confirm.

This may take a few days to completely propagate. After you have confirmed that the channels have been removed, proceed to delete your child's entire Google+ account. Google began integrating services into Google+ without users' consent. This has led to much confusion about how the social network should be used. However, much of your child's personal details are likely present on some layer of this service. The directions below will completely close the Google+ profile.

- Navigate to **google.com/account** and select "Data tools" in the menu.

- Under the "Account management" section, click "Delete Google+ profile."

Instagram

Instagram makes account deletion easy. There is no need to remove individual posts or content. The following steps should permanently remove your child's entire profile from the Internet.

- Navigate to **Instagram.com/accounts/remove/request/permanent.**

- Select any option from the dropdown menu explaining the reason for deletion, and click "Permanently delete my account."

Summary

Throughout this chapter we've explained how parents can easily establish online rules and launch important discussions with their kids. In addition, the search tools and reporting strategies will ensure moms and dads are well prepared to take the necessary next steps if an online situation escalates. While we've armed you with some excellent strategies within the first ten chapters of *Outsmarting Your Kids Online*, we also highly recommend a couple of websites that provide timely and relevant resources for parents on the digital front.

The first of these resources is the US-based *Common Sense Media* (**commonsensemedia.org**), which we've referenced a number of times. This organization rates, educates, and advocates for kids, families, and schools. There is probably no better place on the Internet to find age-appropriate content and apps. Plus, they have in-depth advice for parents, educators, and kids. While we're focused extensively on technology for a younger generation, this site also recommends top picks insofar as books if your child needs a break from the online world.

The second resource is Canada-based *MediaSmarts* (**mediasmarts.ca**). This organization focuses on digital and media literacy. While not as in-depth as *Common Sense Media* on the reviews front, they have an excellent section featuring digital issues such as excessive Internet use, online hate, sexting, gambling, and much more. We also recommend parents follow both of these organizations on Twitter @CommonSense and @MediaSmarts. Both accounts are updated daily with the latest news and information about helping families to make smart technology choices. In our final chapter, we'll talk about tomorrow's challenges, including what you need to know about advances in connected devices of all kinds that will affect our privacy and security.

A Question from a Parent

Josh Dyan: My "what keeps you up at night" issues revolve around YouTube celebs and Minecraft. So many issues around with that I don't know where to start. We trust Sienna online and she knows right from wrong and asks whenever she feels there is a grey area. But the truth is Minecraft and YouTube consume a ton of her time, and I just don't know what we don't know.

Amber's Answer: We've been repeatedly mentioning throughout the book that not all content is created equal; we can say the same thing for YouTube celebrities. Depending on Sienna's age, you may want to consider YouTube's Kids app as it does include many of the online personalities that today's children love to watch. For example, 25-year-old Joseph Garrett (AKA stampylonghead) is just one example of a well-known online personality who focuses on providing educational content for his fans. In fact, he often partners with other organizations to create PG videos that will teach kids how to build in Minecraft in new and exciting ways (he is so successful that he even has his own online retail store with products featuring his brand!). While there is no shortage of good quality content like this, the key is to remember the other two Cs we mentioned from Guernsey's book. In other words, take into consideration the context in terms of when your child is watching (has she been on her device all day long without outdoor play?), but also consider other warning signs (is she withdrawing from offline activities that she used to love?). If the answer to both of these questions is yes, you need new boundaries for technology usage.

Chapter Eleven
Tomorrow's Challenges

There is a technology company based in Paris, France best known for an innovative new product called Pepper. With a name like this, you might think that Pepper is an app, a gadget, or a computer. In many ways, you could say all three are true. *Aldebaran* designs humanoid robots; Pepper is one of its latest creations.

To get a sense of its physical appearance, think of a friendly-looking robot the height of a six-year-old child, complete with big, expressive eyes and a state-of-the-art tablet on its chest. What's special about Pepper, aside from speaking four languages and other remarkable features, is that it can identify emotions. From joy to sadness, from anger to surprise, it is programmed to determine its owner's mood. Moreover, Pepper gets smarter over time as it gets to know you better. Yes, while some fancy new robots are built to do housework, such as vacuuming and washing dishes, Pepper's main job is pretty simple—and pretty important—to keep people happy.

Since it is connected to the Internet, Pepper is able to engage in conversations with you, find information for you, and keep you entertained. With artificial intelligence, this robot will be able to do many of the things—emotionally—that humans do. If you think about it, without letting the inevitable image of evil robots taking over the world seep into your head, it's not difficult to dream up a wide range of possibilities for Pepper; especially as the company behind it is planning to launch a massive app ecosystem, so the robot can be increasingly useful for both specific businesses and consumer needs.

For starters, Pepper is already greeting customers at more than 140 SoftBank mobile retail stores in Japan. While this means human greeters are losing work, there are still humans present who are required to perform more traditional customer support (more traditional than simply posing for selfies, which is a common Pepper request!).

Eventually, individual families will adopt Pepper (or a similar humanoid robot) to keep them entertained in their homes. Imagine, for example, how such a robot could help to keep a lonely elderly person company—especially, as Aldebaran says on their website, "Pepper gradually memorizes your personality traits, your preferences, and adapts himself to your tastes and habits."

Pepper also has an anti-collision system so it can keep its balance. It has a sophisticated network of sensors that allow it to play games, and it is equipped to recognize its owner's voice.

We mention the future of robotics as just one example of how things are going to evolve, and more rapidly than we ever imagined. While we are, in this book, focusing on today's landscape, the risks we've discussed, including privacy and security, primarily address what kids are currently doing with their phones, tablets, and computers. In fact, it's difficult for many parents to imagine a world where these products aren't front and center, endlessly distracting children from the reality in front of them. However, that new connected world is coming.

Remember, we are at the very beginning of the technological revolution. What we see around us right now in terms of innovation is just a tiny sliver of what we can expect 5, 10, or 25 years down the road. Think about some of the companies you are doing business with today. These bullets from the agency Wetpaint MENA showcase how they're using technology to disrupt the world's economy:

- Uber: The world's largest taxi company owns no vehicles
- Facebook: The world's most popular media creates no content
- Alibaba: The world's most valuable retailer has no inventory
- Airbnb: The world's largest lodging provider owns no real estate

To prepare you for this rapidly changing future, which is progressing more quickly in some parts of the world than others, we need to restate that what we will all have to manage on the technology front goes well beyond just the tiny screens in our hands.

After we plunge into this next big tech trend, called the Internet of Things (and yes, Pepper falls into this category), we will wrap up this section with some important hands-on advice that includes the final strategies and tools you need today to monitor what your kids are doing online.

Internet of Things (IoT)

Early in 2015, the online world was abuzz with stories about select models of Smart TVs spying on consumers. Similar to Apple's Siri voice recognition program, which allows you to speak into your iPhone to perform certain tasks, a few particular models of Samsung televisions launched with built-in speech features so you can do something similar. For example, you could say, "Hi TV" and request your favorite channel using your voice.

Within the company's privacy policy, Samsung recommends that you "be aware that your spoken words include personal or other sensitive information, that information will be among data captured and transmitted to a third party through your use of Voice Recognition." This essentially means that if you have this feature enabled, anything you say on command will be uploaded to a third-party service to fulfill that command.

Connected televisions live within one tiny category of products that are defining the future of the Internet of Things. This is a big term that includes any product or device connected to the Internet. The average family has most likely ignored this massive technology trend; probably because it lacks one common operating system, and is consequently absent of a proper comprehensive marketing approach.

According to a recent Gartner report, 26 billion devices will be connected to the Internet by 2020. Much of this growth will be in the area of consumer products, "things" that are built smart just for you. Let's take a look at another example of such a product.

Oombrella is an unforgettable umbrella, according to the company that makes it. It's not unforgettable just because of its unique, shiny, and colorful exterior, but because it is smart. Within the handle of this connected product, there is a mini weather station that collects data including temperature, pressure, humidity, and light. Through the app on your smartphone, you can see these forecasts which are shared with other Oombrella owners. If you leave your Oombrella behind, it will send you a message to return to pick it up where you left it.

Connected TVs and umbrellas are just the beginning. Below are a few IoT verticals that will massively affect you and your family over the next few years. While we are enthusiastic about many of the technologies below, we're also concerned about the extensive privacy and security challenges that these products present.

The Future of Toys

Barbie's maker is determined to make her smart—not in terms of her IQ, but instead in terms of her connectivity. No, this model didn't launch an exciting new career as a scientist or astronaut. Instead, "Hello Barbie" is the company's first connected doll. Her microphone records kids talking to her, so she can send the information to the Internet, via WiFi, to process what they're saying. Then she responds accordingly. Privacy advocates campaigned to get this trendy new toy removed from stores, worried she would record and store intimate conversations with kids.

As Mattel's Michelle Chidoni explains to *PRWeek.com* in response to the backlash: "When we launched Hello Barbie, we wanted to hide nothing, so we created a huge website with an education tool about how the doll works, what she does and doesn't do, [and outlined] safety requirements and safety policies." Chidoni adds, "All of that being said, Hello Barbie is still a headline because [Internet safety] is a bigger issue beyond Barbie."

Yes, Internet safety is a big issue, especially when it comes to businesses that market to kids. Another company that is leading the way with connected toys is VTech. They too recently showed up in the hacking headlines. In November of 2014, 4.8 million customers had their personal details stolen. Since kids are the primary users of their interactive products, this means preschoolers' private data, including names, birth dates, addresses, and more, was leaked online.

The Future of Health

You probably remember many sleepless nights when your child was an infant. Every parent recalls those stressful moments, standing over your baby boy or baby girl watching him or her breathe to make sure their child is OK. Mimo promises to end this inevitable parent trend. Thanks to a tiny plastic high-tech turtle that's built into each of the company's custom sleepers, you can get information on your smartphone about your baby's breathing, body position, sleep activity, and more. Mimo states on their website that they use low-power Bluetooth Low energy and it is safe for your baby. This sleeper can also send live audio, so you can hear your child throughout the night, using the app.

For adults, the IoT healthcare products and programs are also plenty. John Hancock recently launched their VITALITY initiative so that customers can prove–using technology–that they are embracing healthy living. How do they do this? If you're using a wearable fitness product such as a FitBit or an Apple Watch, you can earn points if you stay active. Subsequently, these points could land you a discount on your insurance. There is also a wide range of new products that will monitor your glucose levels, heart rate, body posture, and much more. The IoT market for healthcare and monitoring products is expected to exceed $117 billion by 2020.

The Future of Shopping

If you think selfies are just for fun, keep an eye on what MasterCard is doing to make these selfies useful. For payment verification, the company is using facial recognition so that you can prove it's actually you buying something (yes, smile...and pay!). As CNBC writes in reference to this trend, "Biometric solutions could include facial recognition, fingerprint scanners, or checking the customer's heartbeat using wearable technology such as smartwatches."

On the topic of passwords, while a world without passwords might seem attractive, we have to think about what areas of our privacy and security we're compromising.

Take beacons, for example, which are tiny pieces of hardware that operate via Bluetooth to send messages to smartphones. In the context of shopping, as you walk into your favorite clothing store you could receive a notification when you enter about a flash sale that's in the works for the next ten minutes. Of course, it would require you to opt in to receive these messages through the store's app, but it's easy to imagine how quickly this will be invasive. For starters, it's safe to say that all retailers want to collect data about your engagement in their stores so they can track customer behavior. While you might want to believe these retailers are protecting your privacy, we know it's hard for all of them to meet a high quality standard.

The Future of Transportation

We chuckle about the rise of driverless cars, but the industry is quickly heading in this direction. Google is leading the way, currently testing its autonomous vehicles on streets in the United States (with passengers "parked" inside to take over if something goes wrong). The company is also working with Congress to regulate the industry, arguing that inconsistent state laws make it difficult for Google to innovate on this front. Today, there is a lot more technology in cars than most of us want to accept. In fact, most manufacturers build automobiles that are connected to the Internet. Any given week you will read articles discussing how easy it is for a car to be hacked.

The Future of Homes

While you will increasingly encounter IoT products in the verticals above, it's the connected home that will affect you and your kids today. These products include technology such as Nest, which allows you to better manage the temperature in your home from your smartphone. Another popular product is the Kevo Smart Lock, which lets you open your door from your smartphone (and create digital keys for anyone in your contacts). If we look again to the year 2020, the Smart Homes Market by Product research study says the industry will reach more than $58 billion.

We could go on forever about the potential IoT opportunities and challenges. Again, when it comes to your children, this new trend means that your job to protect them will require tech knowledge well beyond basic use of smartphones, tablets, and computers. To give you a bit more insight into potential IoT dangers, Michael's Hack will showcase the world's first search engine for Internet-connected devices.

Your child's computers, laptops, tablets, and cellular telephones are not the only digital devices that are targeted by malicious hackers and pedophiles. Practically everything that we do today involves a computer network. Your home security systems probably have a data connection to some network. Many of you may even possess a home thermostat that is connected to the Internet. Practically every piece of technology created today can connect to either a wired or wireless Internet connection. New televisions connect in order to stream programming while wireless surveillance cameras connect to provide a live view from your mobile device. External hard drives connect to share files between several computers. This trend is not going away soon. Amazing new technologies have revolutionized the way we live our daily lives. They have also created huge vulnerabilities waiting to be exploited by bored technology enthusiasts. We must be more cautious than ever when we connect new devices to networks. A default or inappropriate configuration can make the device visible to the world through the Internet without you or your child knowing. There is probably someone scanning for various devices to connect to the Internet right now.

Surveillance Cameras

Searching for vulnerable devices on the Internet is quite easy. For many years, specific searches on Google would identify various types of hardware waiting for a connection. This is often referred to as "Google hacking." In 2005, a very popular search was for Everfocus brand digital surveillance systems that were connected to the Internet. This was a new feature that allowed you to view your home or business video security system from any web browser. If you were traveling, you could use the hotel computer to view live video and make sure everything was fine, and that your child was safe. Any system that you buy today has this capability.

At the time, a search on Google for "intitle:everfocus.EDSR.applet" would link you to thousands of these affordable security systems with a direct connection through the Internet. Once connected, you would be prompted for a user name and password. A quick Google search for the Everfocus user manual revealed the default user name was "admin" and the default password was "admin." Some models used a password of "111111." Almost every unit that could be connected to had the default password in place. One could instantly view live video from homes and businesses worldwide. What about today?

This outdated and insecure digital video recorder is still in use. At the time of this writing, there were 710 of them still available through Google. We picked ten random results and attempted the "admin/admin" combination. Eight of them were successful and allowed us to view the live video feed.

The primary feature of this device is the ability to monitor the video feed remotely. Removing the device from the Internet will eliminate this benefit. The vulnerability here is the weak password. If the users of these systems changed the default user names and passwords, access would be much more difficult. This specific search is only one of thousands in the Google Hacking Database that is maintained at **www.exploit-db.com/google-dorks**.

Hard Drives

Many external hard drives are actually Network Attached Storage (NAS) devices. You can connect a network cable from your home router into the back of the device and make the disk available to your child or anyone on your network. This is convenient for accessing your data from any desktop or laptop in your home. Unfortunately, some people simply plug them in without properly configuring the security of the device. If you do this, search engines will pick up on it. A search of "iomega country:us" revealed 5,169 online devices in the United States made by Iomega, an external hard drive manufacturer. Most results connect directly to an individual's hard drive without any credentials needed and provide complete access to a page of files and folders.

Thermostats

Several years ago, programmable thermostats were all the rage. Today, it is rare to find a home without one. The newest gadget is the wireless digital thermostat that connects to the Internet. A smartphone app can control the temperature while you are away, to save on utility bills. This is fascinating technology that is begging to be hacked. A search online of "Netmonitor" "- Login" revealed 686 homes using Heatmiser programmable thermostats in the United Kingdom. There are different brands popular in the United States, but we did not want to give anyone any ideas. The default user name and password for these devices is "admin / admin." Of the twenty devices we tested, eighteen granted us full access. Only two had changed the default password.

Webcams

A typical webcam that is attached to your computer through a USB connection is not connected directly to the Internet. However, newer devices include options to broadcast a webcam directly to an Internet stream. Some people who enable this feature forget about it and it broadcasts any time the computer is on. There are many search options for finding these devices. Our favorite is "webcamxp." This will present hundreds of online webcams in the United States that do not require a password for viewing.

Home Automation & Alarm Systems

This may be the most disturbing online vulnerability. Several new devices have been released that act as a home security system, automation controller, and security camera viewer. These single units look similar to a small computer tablet and hang on a wall in your home. They connect to your wireless network and interact with the home alarm, surveillance cameras, the heating and cooling system, light controllers, and motion detectors. Many people connect them without enabling a password. Each device has a built-in web server that allows users to control it anywhere in their home or on the Internet. Most products supply an app that can allow access from a smartphone.

During our research, we connected to twenty online "Tuxedo" home automation systems made by Honeywell. Only two of them were protected with a password. The remaining were completely open connections that could be accessed from anywhere. Some examples displayed systems that were "Armed Away" indicating the residents were not at home. If we were burglars, this would be a great way to find out when we should break into those homes. This specific system would sound an alarm if entered; however, there is an option to disarm the system by simply clicking one button within the remote access. A smart burglar will access this online utility and disarm the system before entering. A very smart burglar will also decrease the temperature of the house before entering in order to have a cool environment.

Physically identifying this house may prove to be difficult. However, it is not impossible. One of the eighteen devices that we successfully connected to was located in Decatur, Illinois. We know this because of the IP address assigned to the device. Viewing the outdoor security cameras from this system displayed enough details to identify the exact house. We used the Google Maps street view to confirm the address.

We could fill an entire book with these types of examples. A chapter could be written on how hackers have used this technique to gain access to public water supply pumps, red light enforcement cameras, and VOIP telephone systems. Instead, we believe the focus should be on identifying and correcting your own vulnerabilities. Only a professional test of your network will identify every problem. However, a few simple steps will let you know if you have obvious issues that need immediate attention.

The most important lesson here is to enable strong passwords. Leaving the default credentials or no password will allow anyone access. If a criminal does not want to hunt down an original manual to your device, he or she can visit websites such as routerpasswords.com to quickly identify the default password settings. This free service provides quick access for technicians to the default passwords used on routers, web logins, CCTV systems, and other electronic devices. A large portion of their users are curious hackers trying to access online systems. You should identify your device on this website and attempt the default password. If you gain access, you know your device is vulnerable. Refer to your user manual and change the login information.

Putting It All Together

Many parents reading about these interesting search techniques might be worried about their own vulnerabilities associated with the gadgets attached to their home networks. You may be asking yourself "How does all of this apply to my child?" Consider the following ways that your child could be exploited by the techniques mentioned previously.

Surveillance/Web Cameras: If a predator can access your home surveillance cameras or your child's web cam, he or she can peek into your home at any time. This may escalate the desires to attack your child.

Hard Drives: If a predator can access your family's networked hard drives, he or she can access sensitive documents that may lead to blackmail.

Thermostats/Home Automation: If a predator can access these systems, they can potentially be disabled altogether. This often includes electronic locks.

You may now wonder how you could replicate these searches in order to raise awareness with your friends and family and convince them to take action to protect their own devices. Most of the previous searches mentioned here were conducted on the website Shodan. The next section will provide some popular searches that should convince anyone to tighten the security of their online devices.

Michael's Hacks

Shodan (**www.shodan.io**) is a search engine that lets you find specific types of computers, such as routers, servers, and online devices, using a variety of filters. Some have also described it as a search engine of service banners, which are metadata that a device sends back to a client when connected. This can be information about the device software, what options the service supports, a welcome message, or anything else the client would like to know before interacting with the device. In plain English, Shodan can identify vulnerable devices that should not be publicly visible. Many of these may be located inside your home.

The following are search terms that you can enter on the Shodan website. Clicking the resulting links will likely take you directly to an active page for the product or service. If you are prompted to enter a user name and password, please don't. In many states and provinces, this is considered a crime of computer intrusion.

Webcams: These will often display live feeds from computer webcams.

Webcam
Cam
Cams
Netcam
Webcamxp
Webcam7
IP Cam

Security Cameras: These will often display home security camera feeds.

port:554 has_screenshot:true
Everfocus
IP Camera
view/index.shtml

Home Automation: These often control lights, locks, and temperature.

Thread -401 -login
threadx home.html

Future Monitoring

Now that you have secured your child's digital presence, you must continually monitor the entire Internet for any new information that may surface. Recent studies have identified over 55 billion web pages in existence. The hard way to do this would be to scour Google every day looking for anything new identifying your child's information. Do not worry, this monitoring can be automated.

Google Alerts

Google is a very powerful search engine. It can identify areas where your child's personal information, such as name, social networks, and home address, are on display in a public website. Manually searching every week or month is a burden. Google Alerts, located at **google.com/alerts**, can automate this search and send you an email when any new results appear. This free service will basically notify you when your child's information has appeared on a public site.

To use the service, log into your Gmail account. If you do not have a Gmail account, navigate to gmail.com and create a new free account. Navigate to google.com/alerts and determine the exact searches of your child's personal information that would return appropriate results. This will vary depending on how common your child's name is. For example, if his or her name is unique, such as Michael Bazzell, his email address is mbazzell@gmail.com, and you live at 4054 Aberdeen Street in Biloxi, MS, you should create the following alerts.

"Michael Bazzell"
"mbazzell@gmail.com"
"Michael Bazzell" "Aberdeen"
"4054 Aberdeen" "Bazzell"

The quotes should be included in the alert. If you have a child named James, you should also add an alert for him such as "James Bazzell" "Aberdeen." However, if your child has a common name, you will need to add more data. If you do not specify the exact search that you want, you will receive too many false positives for pages that are not about your child. If your child's name is Michael Bazzell, and you live at 1212 Main in Denver, CO, you should create alerts that are specific to this. These should include interests, school name, or associations. The goal is to search for the perfect amount of data to identify your child's public personal leaks without receiving irrelevant data. You will need to manipulate these searches until you achieve only the results that are about him or her.

"Michael Bazzell" "1212 Main" "Denver"
"Michael Bazzell" "volleyball" (specific interest)
"Michael Bazzell" "Denver" "Johnson Middle School" (school)
"Michael Bazzell" "Denver" "Colorado Marching Band" (association)

If your landline telephone number is 314-555-1234 and your child's cellular number is 713-555-9999, you should add the following Google Alerts.

"314-555-1234"
"314" "555-1234"
"713-555-9999"
"713" "555-9999"

These specific search terms will attempt to locate information placed within websites that match the terms inside quotes. For example, if a social network site created a new profile in the name of Michael Bazzell, Google would pick up on this and let you know. If a reverse telephone directory listed the term "Michael Bazzell" and the street of "Main" in the same page, this service would alert you. The quotes mandate that a result is only returned when those words are next to each other on the page. The telephone number examples would identify a website with your child's number even if the area code was separated from the rest of the number.

Now that you have an understanding of how Google Alerts monitors online activity, let's create some together. Navigate to google.com/alerts. Supply the first alert that you want to create. The result type should be "Everything"; frequency should be "As-it-happens"; results should be "All results"; and the delivery should be to your email address. As you create the alert, you will see the current search results in the right column. Click "Create Alert" when complete and continue to add alerts. Click on the "Manage your alerts" button and review your alert settings. Here, you can modify or delete an alert that you have created.

With a properly configured set of Google Alerts, you can be notified in real-time as Google finds information about your child and your family. You are not limited to these examples. We have alerts in place for our websites and books. If any website links to our websites, or someone is discussing our other books, we can be automatically notified and provided a link to the source.

Covert Active Monitoring

Passively monitoring the Internet with the help of Google Alerts may not be enough for some parents. If your child is already experiencing difficulties with online interactions, you may need to increase your surveillance. This is especially true if you suspect that your child is instigating some of the exposure that you have detected. While we ask you to seriously consider whether covertly spying on your child's Internet use is appropriate, we want to offer solutions for parents who need this level of monitoring. We will present this section in two components: computers and mobile devices. The way that you monitor each varies drastically.

Monitoring your child's computer usage on a home computer is relatively easy. Since you likely own the device, and your child is a minor, you have every right to eavesdrop on his or her online activity. This is usually done through parental monitoring software. There is an abundance of this type of software available for free and minimal cost, but we will only focus on one free solution. While we are not affiliated with the program K9 Web Protection, and we do not claim that it is the best solution for your needs, it has one of the longest track records in this category of application. Also, it is free, and works with both Windows and Mac computers.

K9 Web Protection (**k9webprotection.com**) is a free parental control software application that offers many features for monitoring Internet activity and blocking inappropriate websites. Although it is user-friendly and ideal for parents who are not tech-savvy, there are several things that must be considered before putting it to use. We will highlight the three most relevant features.

Monitor Browsing History: With K9 Web Protection, you can know what your child does online. You can identify what types of websites he or she visits most, and how long the activity lasts. This will disclose the online places that your child has a presence and will encourage you to begin monitoring all of the accounts via the Internet.

Block Inappropriate Websites: This software allows you to block any website desired or entire categories of unwanted content. This allows you to choose the level of blockage with descriptions such as alcohol, drugs, nudity, and violence.

Manage Usage Time: K9 Web Protection gives you control of your child's access to the Internet. You can set a weekly, daily, or hourly schedule for using the Internet and prevent access during non-approved times.

There are many limitations with this software and most other similar programs. First, it will only protect your computers within your home. It does nothing to protect your child on devices at school or friends' houses. Next, it does not log everything that your child types into the computer. It is not a traditional key logger and does not email you files displaying every letter pressed on a keyboard. While solutions like this exist, most are borderline viruses that would also obtain your keystrokes, including banking credentials and personal messages. We believe that a solution such as K9 Web Protection provides an adequate amount of security for most families that require active monitoring.

We believe that parental control software for your child's smartphone is likely more vital than the home computer. Overall, kids are more hesitant to make intentional bad choices when using a computer owned by their parents. Most feel a higher likelihood of getting caught when conducting inappropriate activity. When using their own smartphone, they usually feel more freedom and less likelihood of getting busted. While K9 Web Protection offers Android and iPhone apps, we cannot recommend them due to the ease of bypassing the protection with minimal effort. If you have a desire to monitor your child's smartphone activity, we recommend the following.

Monitoring Apps

We should stress once again that there are varying opinions about using apps to monitor your kids online. While there are a number of parents who are against this tactic, claiming that it's an invasion of a child's privacy, we know that there are many scenarios that warrant parents actively stepping in to keep kids safe.

The primary fear when it comes to your children on the Internet is stranger danger, but there are plenty of other reasons that you might want to stay in the loop in terms of their digital activities. As we mentioned earlier on in the book, with kids getting smartphones when they are as young as 6 years old, it's worth learning quick and easy tips to protect them. Also, your reasons for monitoring are going to evolve as your child gets older.

For the youngest kids at home, your child's location is probably the most important feature you will want from one of these apps. As they get into the preteen years, you will want to see how responsibly they're communicating on social media sites, such as Instagram. These good habits early on will teach them better habits when they get into their teen years. For teens, you may have reasons to view their messages if you are worried about their overall well-being. Here are three popular apps that can help you with all of the above.

MamaBear (iOS / Android) **www.mamabearapp.com**

Although this app does allow you to monitor, we also like its focus on family communication. That means that within the Family News section you can coordinate conversations such as soccer pick-ups or school carpools. Similar to the apps below, there is also a focus on social media monitoring, so you will be notified when kids upload publicly online to certain sites such as Instagram and Tumblr. It will also flag inappropriate language and bullying. To monitor text messages on Android devices (only), you will see incoming and outgoing texts. For your older teens who are driving, you will get a notification if they are going over the speed limit you set; plus, you can view their speeding history. As a bit of comfort, this app has received a number of awards including the distinction as one of the World's Most Promising New Companies by CNBC. There is a free version of the app, but you might want to try an ad-free premium account to get extended features (6-month access US$24.99).

TeenSafe (iOS / Android) **www.teensafe.com**

More than one million parents currently use this app. This cross-platform download lets moms and dads monitor activity on Instagram, including posts, comments, and followers. You will also be able to see SMS and iMessages, logs of sent and received calls, location history, current device location, web browsing details, and contact information. If you have more than one teen at home, you can add them to your account (7 Day Free Trial, US$14.95/month). One note about TeenSafe, there are features (similar to MamaBear) that are specifically available if your child is an iPhone user or an Android user. For example, if your daughter has an Android device, you can view a list of third-party apps. If your son has an iPhone, you can view his Kik messages–both sent and received. TeenSafe also has a helpful Parent's Guide that explains why monitoring makes sense. It includes stats such as this: 61 percent of teens have sent nude pictures because they were pressured to do it and over half of all teens have been bullied online.

Visr.co (http://visr.co)

What's interesting about Visr is that it monitors and highlights exclusively for safety issues. In other words, they are less worried about spying on kids' everyday conversations, but instead focused on notifying parents if there are issues such as bullying, explicit content, violence, drugs, and more (in fact there are 22 alert categories). They employ data scientists to best prioritize what parents need to know. Currently, they conduct this monitoring on Instagram, Gmail, YouTube, Facebook, Twitter, Pinterest, and KidsEmail, and are working to add more. As they explain on their website, the average parent will receive about 20 important alerts every single month. The app is currently free, but there is a paid version in the works. For all of the above apps, check out their privacy policies to fully understand what safeguards they put in place in terms of how your information is collected and shared.

Summary

If we look at today's technology icons, we see a consistent trend in terms of their history. Microsoft founder Bill Gates is just one example. He was 13 years old when he started pursuing computer programming, eventually co-founding Microsoft when he was twenty. Facebook founder Mark Zuckerberg has a similar story, starting to code when he was 12 years old. At 20, he launched thefacebook.com. According to *Forbes*, Gates is currently worth about $79.2 billion and Zuckerberg is worth about $47.5 billion–not bad for a couple of high school geeks. While 12 and 13 seem like pretty young ages for computer programming, think about today's tech-savvy children. In many countries around the world, as we mentioned earlier on in the book, coding is now part of elementary school curriculum.

Estonia, which is home to more than one million people, was one of the first places to pilot such as a project. In 2012, they announced that all students from Grades 1 through 12 would learn how to program, studying how to create web and mobile applications. The initiative, called ProgeTiiger, launched with specific guidelines for three phases of school.

In the early years, students learn how to create very simple games (using coding apps that we've discussed, such as ScratchJr). In the middle school years, the focus shifts to more complex projects. During this phase they learn how to program robots and create websites. In high school, they move on to even more complicated work learning how to create high-end web applications. It's no surprise that this country is moving forward aggressively on this front. For a tiny place, they have a big history of innovation (they are, after all, best known as the birthplace of Skype–which Microsoft bought in 2011 for $8.5 billion). The following is from *The Economist* in an article on Estonia in 2013.

"In 2007 it became the first country to allow online voting in a general election. It has among the world's zippiest broadband speeds and holds the record for start-ups per person. Its 1.3 million citizens pay for parking spaces with their mobile phones and have their health records stored in the digital cloud. Filing an annual tax return online, as 95 percent of Estonians do, takes about five minutes."

We mention Estonia and the acceleration of programming in schools because this 21st-century language is the foundation for many IoT products. While we addressed the Internet of Things from a privacy and security standpoint above, we also recognize the opportunities for families. Like a young Bill Gates or Mark Zuckerberg, today's kids are already starting to tinker with their own IoT projects. However, they are not in their preteen or teen years when doing so; many are just fresh out of kindergarten.

If you follow the Twitter handle @IoT4Kids, you will see plenty of examples of how this tinkering is well underway. The account is managed by the creators of the O Watch, which is a smart watch kit for children to learn about programming and 3D printing. In their promo video, a nine-year-old boy describes how he started his first Arduino project when he was 6 years old. He explains how an Arduino micro-controller makes it easy to build simple electronics projects. If you search the site *PopularMechanics.com*, you will see that some examples of other Arduino DIY creations include battery testers, stopwatches, and keypad locks. There are an endless number of things that can be done with this open-source platform. While it might sound intimidating to parents, it's second nature for The Screeners to be able to dive right into the creative process.

The O Watch has compass, temperature, and humidity sensors inside. As an Arduino-based product, you can build games and much more. There is also a community built around this kit so you can learn how to print a 3D case and share your experiments with other kids (AKA makers). The base product includes the following components: 3D printed watch case, color screen with Arduino Zero process, battery, and a band kit (US$69). You can read more about the O Watch and other creative ideas for kids in the Family section of sites such as *MakeZine.com*.

In fact, as you stress about finding the ideal March Break and Summer Camps for your kids, most larger cities now offer some form of maker camps to encourage kids to build, tinker, create, and repeat. Toronto-based *SteamLabs.ca* is just one organization that manages camps for kids as young as six. In the summer they have one-week programs that include everything from sessions detailing how to make robotic ears to teaching kids how to design programmable LED art. In their words, "we'll help you make your crazy ideas happen." Yes, gone are the days when camps were all about swimming and soccer. In fact, your sons and daughters have probably already built something that could be considered an IoT project without you even knowing.

What we've outlined above is one of the most exciting technology opportunities that exists today, the opportunity to create with your kids in a language they understand. If you can work with them to teach them how to build these unique projects, there is no stopping their potential as the future designers and inventors of IoT. Sure, researching the maker space takes time, but the Internet is filled with excellent free resources that are geared to learners of all levels. *GeekDad.com* is yet another example of a site that can help (and don't worry, there is stuff for moms as well!). One of the most recent featured projects is how to make a FlexBot DIY Camera Drone. Kids of all ages will agree this is pretty darn cool!

While parents might see their role in the home as the technology police, reframing this relationship so you are a technology partner can help to build an important connection with your child. If you dream up an exciting how-to project, such as we have outlined above, you will earn their respect. In short, while monitoring apps for both computers and smartphones might be a necessity to keep your son or daughter safe from today's online dangers, your role as a parent can offer opportunities where you can have a productive and positive impact when it comes to tomorrow's technology–starting today.

A Question from a Parent

Sarawr: When my oldest gets grounded from electronics for inappropriate use, she just uses a friend's cellular phone or school computer. How can I explain to her, in a way that matters, that she needs to be more cautious even when I'm not around, to keep her safe?

Amber's Answer: This is an ongoing conversation. As much as she feels frustrated that you keep bringing this up, remind her that you are concerned about her overall well-being. Also, the more you can educate her with current relevant news about risks, the better. Sometimes kids won't believe their parents, but they will believe another source. In fact, you could also consider approaching a slightly older (than your child) family friend or relative who you know she trusts (and admires). Work with that person so you have a third party involved in the conversation to keep firm on your guidelines for all technology inside and outside the home.

Conclusion

When we talk about today's landscape in Chapter One, we refer to the star of a viral video on YouTube. As a reminder, she is a one-year-old child who assumes magazines operate the same way as iPads. In 2025, she will be 14 years old. As a young teen, her world will be even more confusing than it is for kids today. As Pew Internet Center describes in their research on *Digital Life in 2025*, "Experts predict the Internet will become 'like electricity' — less visible, yet more deeply embedded in people's lives for good and ill." The article proceeds to describe some of the less-hopeful scenarios that we should expect, writing that "Abuses and abusers will 'evolve and scale.' Human nature isn't changing; there's laziness, bullying, stalking, stupidity, pornography, dirty tricks, crime, and those who practice them have new capacity to make life miserable for others." They also explain that people will trade convenience over privacy, and comment that only the upscale (AKA the rich) will enjoy real privacy.

As we described in the previous chapter, parents will continue to worry about handheld devices and social media (whatever that might be called) in 2025, but equally concerning will be virtual reality, augmented reality, artificial intelligence, 3D printing, the Internet of Things, and many other innovations. While we are sold the dream that technology will make our lives more simple, we are simultaneously living the reality that technology makes our lives more complicated. However, it's not all gloom and doom. While we talk about many of the risks today and in the future, that's because this book is meant to highlight Internet safety and security concerns–and provide easy-to-implement strategies to combat them. We could also write an entire book on the benefits of technology for children of all ages.

Let's look back to a few of the social networks we mentioned in the earlier chapters. Take Facebook, for example. If you are hunting for educational resources on Zuckerberg's baby, they're not hard to find. Charity: water is one example of an organization that leverages this platform to bring visitors on a journey as they work to bring clean drinking water to more than 600 million people in need. Aside from static posts, they've recently integrated 360-degree videos so you can explore interactive and immersive content on your phone. Simply use your finger to move around the story to get an expanded view, showcasing hidden corners of the video. To take things even further, drop your phone into a virtual reality headset, such as Samsung

Gear VR, and you can "walk" alongside Selam, a 13-year-old girl from Ethiopia, as she gets access to clean drinking water for the first time. You are brought into her world in a way never before possible without actually traveling to her remote village.

On Twitter and Instagram, we shared with you a number of educational accounts to follow. In fact, we recommend you start using these services today. There is no shortage of good quality content on both platforms. More importantly, if you understand how these work from a user's point of view, you will have a much better chance of helping your children if they run into trouble. On the online video front, there are dozens of applications that offer educational experiences. On *Twitch.tv*, the American Red Cross recently live-streamed a Tubeathon to help families who are victims of house fires. Using the platform and the hashtag #help1family, they educated people about fire risks and accepted SMS donations. Beyond social media, augmented reality, artificial intelligence, 3D printing, and the Internet of Things will all impact us in many positive ways.

There is only an upside to knowing the strategies we outline in this book, many of which we've explained that we hope you never have to use. There is no reason Moms and Dads can't learn as much or more than their children know about how all of these tools and things work. Many schools are already quickly adopting and upgrading technology, from hardware to software, to properly educate and equip children for the future. Remember our Estonia example? Yes, 100 percent of children are learning to code by the age of seven. While there is pressure on countries and schools to step up their digital efforts in order to compete, there is less pressure on parents to do the same.

While we might want to think about that one-year-old girl in the YouTube video as a child who intuitively knows how technology works, any expert will explain that it is of course learned behavior. Another factor is time. While kids dedicate countless minutes, and hours, to experiment with new tech, Moms and Dads are often too busy to jump in to learn. As author Rhodri Marsden says in a post on the *INDEPENDENT*:

"A solid relationship with technology seems to be a function of leisure time, something that parents can be woefully short of. The resulting technological consultation of children by their parents could just be seen as an amusing reversal of authority within the family unit, but it does throw up a number of questions, both financial and moral."

If you've reached the end of our book, you are well-prepared to change that reversal of authority, and you are empowered with information to teach your children about the future of our connected world. When you're *Outsmarting Your Kids Online*, you're resuming your position in the home as a leader and as an educator; and while it might be a thankless job in the beginning, there is nothing more important than your child's safety and security.

Index